Enriching
your
Marriage

Enriching your Marriage

CHOOSING YOUR PARTNER

AND CREATING

A FOREVER MARRIAGE

Clark Swain, PhD

Horizon Publishers
Springville, Utah

© 2011 Clark Swain

ISBN 13: 978-0-88290-966-0

Published by Horizon, an imprint of Cedar Fort, Inc., 2373 W. 700 S., Springville, UT 84663
Distributed by Cedar Fort, Inc., www.cedarfort.com

LIBRARY OF CONGRESS CATALOGING-IN-PUBLICATION DATA

Swain, Clark, author.
  Enriching your marriage / Clark Swain. -- [Second edition]
      p. cm.
  ISBN 978-0-88290-966-0
  1. Marriage. I. Title.
  HQ734.S978 2011
  646.7'8--dc22

                        2011003300

Cover design by Megan Whittier
Cover design © 2011 by Lyle Mortimer
Edited and typeset by Kelley Konzak

Printed in the United States of America

10 9 8 7 6 5 4 3 2 1

Printed on acid-free paper

*I dedicate this book to my best friend, my wife,
and my lover, Eleanor D. Swain, "Ellie D."*

*Dedicated to all people who have the courage and
self-discipline to be true to their marriage partner.*

Contents

Acknowledgments

Thanks to my wife, Eleanor D. Swain, my best friend, for her unwavering loyalty. Ellie D, my darling, and I have been allies for fifty-six years. Utilizing her good judgment and editing skills, Eleanor read the entire manuscript and offered valuable recommendations. She also made valuable contributions to the chapter on divorce by investigating research findings pertaining to divorce and consequential happiness or unhappiness following divorce. The power of love and commitment rock.

I also want to acknowledge our married sons and daughters, who were smart enough to choose marriage partners who are loaded with good qualities and with whom they have happy, strong marriages. Blake and Linda, Dean and Valerie, Carl and Becky, Mike and Jennifer, and to our single son, Joe.

I acknowledge the goodness of my mom and dad and their valuable contribution to my life. Bert Swain was a very good farmer, beekeeper, bricklayer, and stonemason. He was the root of my sense of humor, and from him I also learned to work hard and never give up. My mother, Fern Gerber Swain, taught me to pray and to enjoy speaking at church and anywhere else where people were willing to listen to me.

Megan is our friend and office associate. She is a university marriage, family, and human development graduate with honors. Because of my visual disability, Megan read aloud this entire manuscript with me. Megan was especially helpful because she has autonomy of thought and the courage to express her thoughts and opinions. We edited until we both felt good about it. Megan spoke words of wisdom, and she gave me her input. Whoever wins her heart and hand will be a very lucky guy.

Thanks to our granddaughter Courtney Steele Tam for her research contributions. Courtney is a marriage, family, and human development graduate who demonstrates qualities of being a wife and mother as described in this book.

My special thanks to Heather Holm, managing editor, for her kind help. My special thanks also to Kelley Konzak for her superior editing and typesetting. My sincere thanks to Horizon publishers and Cedar Fort, Inc. and everyone associated with them who have worked cooperatively toward the publication of this book.

Preface

IF YOU ARE married or if you ever intend to marry, this book is especially for you. It is also for anyone who is interested in living a happy, successful life.

You singles who plan to marry need to know the truth about love and the key characteristics of compatible relationships. Knowing this, you can shop more lovingly and more wisely in the market of love for someone you can live happily with all your life.

A false belief about love that is widespread in North America is the idea that intense romantic love during courtship means a couple is sufficiently well-matched to have a happy marriage. Love alone is not enough for a happy marriage. Compatible lifestyles, compatible life goals, compatible personalities, and much more are also necessary. Should you marry your fiancé? Probably so, but perhaps not.

Another mistaken belief about love is the myth that once the glowing flames of a relationship have dwindled to smoldering coals or have gone out entirely, a couple is helpless to rekindle the fire of their relationship. From this book, you can learn how to strike another match and rebuild a warm relationship.

Marriage is the hub of all other relationships in the family; therefore, it must be given high priority. As with engines, most marriages do not need a major overhaul but just a minor tune-up from time to time.

From reading this book, you can learn how to enrich an already good marriage, how to reconcile "irreconcilable differences," and how to turn your love relationship from a downward spiral into an upward spiral. You can also learn the basics of what every good marriage needs, techniques of anger management, and how to help the sexual love in your marriage blossom.

I am often asked to speak to members of civic organizations and to school and church groups. Occasionally, during the question-answer sessions following my talk, someone inquires about the causes of my blindness and the effect it has had on my marriage and on my philosophy of life. For this reason, I have included an article explaining the onset of blindness during my engagement and its influence on my marriage relationship.

Happy individuals, compared to individuals who are unhappy, are more likely to succeed at creating happy relationships. In other words, mental health enhances marital health. You must be "happily married to yourself" if you are to be psychologically capable of contributing to the happiness of others. Being happily married to yourself is an essential prerequisite to being happily married to anyone else. It is the theme of part three of this book, which includes crisis adjustment, decision making, feeling good about taking charge of our emotions, and conquering fear, indecision, and worry.

Decide now what kind of marriage and what kind of life you want. With best wishes to you for happiness in your marriage and success in your life.

Sincerely,

Clark Swain

PART I

The Truth about Love

You will find loving easier and more rewarding if you know the truth about love and how it differs from infatuation. Part one of this book explains the realities of love and guides you in your choice of a marriage partner. The seeds of success or failure in marriage are sown, to a great extent, during the mate selection process. No mate can bring complete happiness to an unhappy person, but your choice of a marriage partner can greatly increase or diminish your happiness. Should you marry your fiancé? Probably so, but maybe not.

1

The Truth about Love

Do you believe you know the truth about love? Maybe you do, but perhaps love is not entirely what you think it is. Here are some facts and fiction about love:

1. **Fiction**: *Being in love is sufficient for a good marriage.*
   Fact: *Love is not enough.* Consider a couple who we'll call Lisa and Roger. Let's say they have most of the ingredients of an "in love" relationship. There are strong romantic and sexual feelings between them. Each admires the other in many ways, and they share many fun activities. But marriage between these lovers would be unwise because they clash in one of their major values and life goals—Roger wants children but Lisa does not.

2. **Fiction:** *There is no way to resist falling in love or to avoid falling out of it.* People who believe this myth allow themselves to fall in and out of love, thinking there's nothing they can do about it.
   Fact: *To start loving a certain person or to stop loving someone is a decision.* I don't mean one just sits down and decides, "Tomorrow I'll look for someone to fall in love with," or "This month I'll fall out of love with my marriage partner." One's decision is more subtle than that. Loving someone means that we treat him or her in certain ways. This requires

conscious effort. We have the power within ourselves to keep loving our present mate or to start loving someone new. Love is a decision. It is a daily decision that needs to be renewed each morning.

3. **Fiction:** *Lovers should follow their feelings of love. Our feelings of love should guide our actions.*

   Fact: *Acting as we feel without thinking often brings hurt and loss.* A couple in their late twenties sat on a couch in front of me. They were the parents of four children, and the husband was successful in a professional career. The wife was considering divorce. "There's nothing really wrong with my husband," she said. "It's just that I don't feel love for him anymore." She now felt love for another man, so she followed her feelings and divorced her husband. Things did not work out between her and the other man. Her lack of education and career training made it difficult for her to get a job. Now there was less money, so she and her children had to move from their house into an apartment. Her life was lonely and without love. This woman then realized that her act of divorce had been more emotional than rational. She sought reconciliation, but her former husband had made another commitment. For more roses than thorns in our bouquets of love, we must add clear thinking to our feelings and not always follow our feelings.

4. **Fiction**: *Feelings of love should always remain the same between partners who are well matched.*

   Fact: *Feelings of love do change between people even though their love is genuine.* As time passes, our feelings change about most things—about our hometown, our occupation, the significance of money, and so on. For example, when I was a high school student, it was very important to me that our ball teams win. Now, many years later, hometown games are of no concern to me. So it is with a love partnership. As time passes, some of its qualities may decrease, while others increase. Time may dull a couple's ability to enjoy hiking and skiing together but may sharpen their ability to understand each other's attitudes and sense of humor. We cannot feel exactly the same way about love—or anything else—as we did years ago.

5.   **Fiction:** *Intense jealousy is a sign of strong love.*

Fact: *A jealous partner often lacks self-confidence, so he fears his mate will lose interest in him and turn to someone else.* If a loved one is actually being untrue, feelings of jealousy are understandable, but jealousy itself is not a sign of love, and it does not improve love. Irrational jealousy has damaged and ruined many love partnerships.

6.   **Fiction:** *Love is blind.*

Fact: *Love is not blind, but some lovers are.* They see qualities in the partner that aren't really there. This is why it has been said that "Love is an insane desire to squeeze orange juice out of a lemon." Always look for your partner's good traits, but don't exaggerate them.

7.   **Fiction:** *Money has nothing to do with love.*

Fact: *A couple's level of income is positively related to their level of marital happiness.* There is a saying that when poverty walks in the door, love flies out the window. Income even seems to be more vital than education in contributing to the happiness of a marriage.

Knowing the truth about love can help us get a good bargain in the marriage market. Combining reality with romance helps us see what is really there in a prospective marriage partner, not more or less. Having learned some of the facts about love, we are also ready to give more to our love relationships. If a marriage is to last, partners must be able to distinguish fiction from facts. Let's remember, loving someone or not loving that person begins with a decision. If we are to love well, we must live well, and we must know the truth about love.

2

Should You Fall in Love

or Walk In?

It's easy to fall in love, and it's exciting. In many parts of the world, being in love is an important prerequisite to marriage. But how can you be sure that you're really in love? What would characterize the relationship between you and your partner if you are in love? In most cases, you would find each other's physical appearance appealing. You would have feelings of mutual affection. Each of you would admire the other in many ways. You would agree more often than disagree and would feel comfortable together so that you could relax and be yourselves. You would enjoy each other's company enough so that when you are apart you'd look forward to being together again. You would be good friends. It has been said that a state of love exists between two persons when each feels toward the other, "I'm all for you, and you're all for me." This portrays a couple in love.

Why do some love partnerships last for more than half a century, while others end in less than half a year? Love endures when a couple is capable in the art of loving.

THE ART OF LOVING

If love partnerships are to endure, lovers must develop skill at the art of loving. We are not born with the ability to love. We must learn it. It's okay to fall in love if we can also walk into a love partnership with knowledge about love and the ability to love. One who has skill at the art of loving is more likely to succeed not only at marriage but in all human relations as well. This is true because loving is a way of treating all people. It is caring, respecting, responding, giving, sharing, and forgiving.

Loving is caring. A man was a day late returning home from a camping trip. His wife was worried about him, so she left a note asking him to phone her office when he returned. He didn't bother to call. It hurt her feelings that he didn't seem to care enough to phone and relieve her anxiety.

How much we care about a certain person shows how much we love that person. And our ability to care about all people is a measure of our ability to love. A loving person cares enough about people that he will not intentionally do anything to harm anyone. Love means we care enough about others to turn our self-centered mirrors into windows. A lover who's all wrapped up in himself makes a small package and is not ready for marriage.

Loving is respecting. The dictionary says to respect is "to value and honor." In loving, we must value people enough to give them the freedom to choose what they will do. It may be necessary at times for an adult to force a child to do something against his wishes, but when two grown people are relating to each other, if there is love between them, there should be no force. Loving is persuading, not forcing.

Loving is responding. It is responding with a smile, a firm hand clasp, and a letter answered promptly. When being introduced, have you ever extended your hand to someone only to get a "lifeless" response? Thinking of it as a hand hug instead of a handshake can remind us to combine firmness with gentleness in the handclasp. Have you ever sent a letter to someone, the kind of letter that deserved a response, and yet you got no answer? Loving is responding.

Loving is giving. It is giving valentines, Easter baskets, and Christmas gifts. But far more important, it is a gift of one's self. Kahlil Gibran said, "You give but little when you give of your possessions. It's when you give of yourself that you truly give."[1] One of the gifts that a father gave to his son for Christmas was a letter that said, "Dear Jimmy, during the coming year I will give you some of my time each day for us to use as you wish."

One satisfying thing about giving love is that love comes back to the lover. This even occurs in the classroom, where a teacher who gives much to his students will find they respond with better attendance and more interest. The more we give the more we get. The good effects of love are not limited to the loved one but promote the happiness and further the development of the loving one as well.

Loving is sharing. When I was a boy on the farm, we had horses for pulling machinery, for driving cattle, and for running in the races at rodeo time. Most of all, I liked our thoroughbred race horses. Each spring, I ask my family to join me at the TV for the Kentucky Derby, Preakness, and Belmont Stakes. If something exciting is about to happen, I want someone there to share the experience. Mark Twain said, "To get the full benefit of joy you've got to find someone to divide it with."[2] Have you ever noticed how joy shared is increased? And how sorrow shared is decreased? Loving is sharing. It is a willingness to share bad times as well as good times.

Loving is forgiving. A loving person forgives one who has wronged him, and he also forgives himself for mistakes he has made. To refuse to forgive is unloving. There may be those who say, "Okay, I'll forgive you, but I'll never forget what you've done." This is just another way of saying, "I won't forgive you."

Also, be willing to forgive yourself for your blunders. To refuse to do so is an unloving act against yourself. If God will forgive you and other people will forgive you, then why shouldn't you forgive yourself?

Loving is knowing how to love ourselves properly. This will improve our ability to love others. Self-love is morally right. The New Testament says "Love thy neighbor as thyself." It does not say, "Love thy neighbor instead of thyself." Proper self-love includes self-acceptance, caring for one's health, and continuing self-improvement. Unwise self-love is really selfishness. It includes self-centeredness and self-indulgence. Loving yourself properly enhances your qualities, and this makes you more lovable.

Real love is basically the same in all human relations, whether between a grandfather and grandmother, a newly married couple, or parent and child. It involves caring, respecting, responding, giving, sharing, and forgiving. Notice that these words are verbs, and verbs denote action. Loving requires action.

The apostle Paul cites the qualities of a person who has developed their ability at the art of loving. In 1 Corinthians 13:4–6 he says, "Love is very patient and kind, never jealous or envious, never boastful or proud. Never haughty or selfish or rude. Love does not demand its own way. It is not irritable or touchy. It does not hold grudges and will hardly even notice when others do it wrong. It is never glad about injustice, but rejoices whenever truth wins out."[3]

COMMITMENT

Commitment means each partner makes a pledge to himself or herself to keep on loving the other even when it's difficult to do so. It's okay to fall in love, but if your love is to last, you must also be able to walk into it with love and a commitment to stay together. Love that endures requires partners who are willing to learn and relearn the art of loving and who have the courage to commit themselves to keep on loving, even when it's difficult.

DIFFERENCES BETWEEN GENUINE LOVE AND INFATUATION

University Students' Comments on Love

Infatuation to me means a strong attraction to another person that is mostly physical. It may be an overwhelming, sudden emotional experience that is one-sided attachment. When I think of infatuation, I think of a feeling one gets from seeing, say, Brad Pitt in a movie. Probably nothing will ever come of it.

Mature love means something else entirely. Love means having respect for another person, having trust and confidence; also it means having a physical closeness—sexual attraction contributes to two people's relationship. But in order for love to survive, there must be more to it than just sex.

A loving relationship adds to one's feelings of security and reassurance.

Debi Lick

The difference between infatuation and mature love . . .

Infatuation is an artificial love. It is based on such things as looks, reputation, and style. . . . These characteristics are not enough to make it a lasting relationship.

Mature love may include some infatuation but also entails more important feelings that go much deeper. These are the feelings that build a lasting relationship. They include such things as companionship, friendship, and self-assurance. These make you feel good not only about the person you love, but about yourself as well.

Laurie Harrison

Differences between Love and Infatuation

Infatuation is instant desire. It is one set of glands calling to another. Love is friendship that has caught fire. It takes root and grows—one day at a time.

Infatuation is marked by a feeling of insecurity. You are excited and eager, but not genuinely happy. There are nagging doubts, unanswered questions, little bits and pieces about your beloved that you would just as soon not examine too closely. It might spoil the dream.

Love is quiet understanding and the mature acceptance of imperfection.

It is real. It gives you strength and grows beyond you—to bolster your beloved. You are warmed by his presence, even when he is away. Miles do not separate you. You want him nearer. But near or far, you know he is yours and you can wait.

Infatuation says, "We must get married right away. I can't risk losing him."

Love says, "Be patient. Don't panic. He is yours. Plan your future with confidence."

Infatuation has an element of sexual excitement.

Love is the maturation of friendship. You must be friends before you can be lovers.

Infatuation lacks confidence. When he's away, you wonder if he's cheating. Sometimes you even check.

Love means trust. You are calm, secure and unthreatened. He

feels that trust, and it makes him even more trustworthy.

Infatuation might lead you to do things you'll regret later, but love never will. Love is an upper. It makes you look up. It makes you think up. It makes you a better person than you were before.[4]

A Pastor's Open Letter to Persons in Love

I love you.

This simple statement can lead to a lot of things: to a kiss, to sharing two lives together as one, to marriage—and to divorce. You see, it largely depends on what we mean when we say the words "I love you."

We are often confused to know what we mean when we talk about "love." I have come to a distinction with regard to two kinds of love that I found helpful: there is a difference between a "because of" love and an "in spite of" love. Let me illustrate: To love someone because of the way you feel when you are with him or her, or to love that someone because of his looks or the way she cooks or the things she does or the things he says is one thing. It is something quite different to love that someone in spite of the fact that he or she has faults.

This distinction is basic: it is the key to having a successful, happy love relationship rather than one that will eventually end up in a hell of a mess. To say "I love you because of what you have or do or how you make me feel, or because I need you" is not saying "I love you" at all! It is saying, "I love me" and "I love you because you have something I want." To say "I love you in spite of your failures and I will no matter what you do" is to say "I give myself."

You see, love begins with a commitment: "I will love you. I will love you in spite of your failures; my commitment to you remains firm." This is the basis for a sound marriage. How different this is from saying "I love you because I feel good when I am with you."

So then, whether you are just beginning to date, going steady, are engaged, or are married, seek to love in spite of. Remember, God loves you, not because you are good or perfect, but in spite of the fact that you are not. You are loved by God, therefore you can love another person in spite of his or her failures. Your love can transform his or her life as well as your own. . . .

Yours in Love
Earl Gibbs, Minister
Springfield Christian Church

NOTES

1. Kahlil Gibran, *The Prophet* (New York: Alfred A. Knopf, 1923).
2. Mark Twain, found through www.goodreads.com.
3. The Layman's Parallel New Testament—The Living New Testament
4. Ann Landers, *Idaho Statesman*, Saturday, February 13, 1982.

3

Is Premarital Sex for You?

To Be or Not to Be

I RESPECT YOUR right to choose your own sexual values and life-style. You are free to decide to be or not to be involved in non-marital sex. Although your sexual beliefs might be very different from mine, I will not judge you or think I am better than you, and I will still want to be your friend.

In writing, counseling, and teaching, I do not have the right to *impose* my values on you or anyone else. I do believe I have the responsibility, however, to *expose* my values to my readers, clients, and students. I also request that you do not judge me or reject me because of my convictions concerning sex.

My Values

I believe that sex is a gift from our creator. It is for procreation, for pleasure, and for power—love power. Nothing can exceed the power of sexual love in strengthening and revitalizing a marriage.

I would caution you about sex not because it is bad, but because it is so good. Depending on how it is used, it can bring both good and bad into your life. Sex can be compared to water and fire. When kept under control, water and fire are good, but they are destructive whenever they are running or burning out of control. I know that self-control doesn't sound like much fun, but please be patient with me and withhold your conclusions until your comprehension is complete.

I believe that sexual love in marriage, as contrasted to sex out of marriage, has the greatest potential for mutual satisfaction and the least potential for emotional turmoil. No one has ever sought counseling from me because of being emotionally disturbed about their virginity. In contrast, a considerable number of individuals have come to me with emotional problems arising from participation in premarital and extramarital sex.

Be Honest with Yourself

Being dishonest with oneself by going further with a dating partner than one wants can diminish one's self-esteem. Inappropriate sexual behavior can also produce subsequent anxiety when relating to an intended marriage partner. This anxiety was experienced by a young man who expressed his opinion as follows:

> I'm sure I was too young. It's a big responsibility. Not only that, it causes a lot of problems between people. When you get that close to somebody, it's never the same again. Never. I don't care how casual it is, it's never the same. You can't just be friends with them anymore. You can't. There's jealousy involved on one side or the other every time. I've never met anybody that you could just have sex with and be like, "Oh, OK, whatever you want. No big deal."

Case Study: Nate and Nancy save sex for marriage

> Nate is "still a virgin" at 25 and says this is due to "my religious beliefs. I believe in commitment and that really sex is a gift for marriage." Nancy said, "I have a real strong feeling about not having sex until I'm married. It's because of my religious beliefs and my upbringing that I feel that way." . . . She has a group of friends who share her beliefs and who have provided mutual support, and now she has a boyfriend who also values virginity before marriage.[1]

"The casual outlook [on sex] tends to ignore the inevitable complications of most sexual relationships. It lapses into a kind of emotional prudery. We are inclined to apply the word prudish to those who deny their sexual being. The modern casualist, however, is an emotional prude; that is, he tries to deny those emotions that cluster around his sexual life."[2]

WHY DOES THE BIBLE TEACH THAT SEX IS ACCEPTABLE ONLY IN MARRIAGE?

The Old and New Testament teachings against adultery and fornication are still valid. I agree with the philosophy of Dr. Charlie Shedd, author of *How to Know if You're Really in Love*, when he says, "It does not matter how we try to bend the laws. Some things remain as God ordained them. And one of these is that sex at its best is not a happening. It is a creation. It is not alone the joining of two bodies. It is the gradual coming together of two lives in their unique response to the goodness of God."[3]

WHAT ARE YOUR VALUES?

What do you believe about sex, and is your sexual lifestyle compatible with your other values? What impact do you think premarital sex and its possible complications would have on your self-esteem? Do you value persons of the other sex as much as you do those of your own gender? How do you value religion and what the Bible teaches about sex? Assuming that you will marry someday, what influence do you think premarital sex might have on the quality of your future marriage? Only you can answer these important questions. You owe it to yourself to give them careful thought and arrive at definite answers. If you are to be happy, you need to *make* things happen in your life, not just *let* them happen.

Your decisions concerning sex before marriage can affect the lives of many people as well as your own. Your family, friends, church, and community have an emotional, moral, or financial investment in your life. Waiting until marriage can lead to more benefits and fewer problems for most couples. I am sure that many young women as well as men hope to find someone who has reserved himself or herself for marriage. Self-esteem that comes from self-discipline and freedom from anxiety and guilt are rewards enjoyed by those who wait.

It's true that more and more young women as well as young men are becoming involved in premarital sex. I wonder how many are trying it out because they think it's the "in thing" to do. Most individuals with a strong religious orientation cannot handle the emotional complications the morning after. Many persons suffer not only feelings of guilt and anxiety but also a loss of self-respect. This loss of self-esteem comes from "following the follower," from doing something mainly because others are doing it.

REWARDS AND PENALTIES

So there are rewards for waiting. Does this mean there are penalties for not waiting? Penalties, if there are any, are mainly self-induced. Guilty feelings come more from a violation of one's own conscience than from society. If one's behavior is different from one's beliefs, guilt feelings usually result. A young man tells this story:

> I had my first experience when I was sixteen. It wasn't good. I think basically because it was like I had won a contest, although I was very careful not to make it seem that way at the time. I had talked a girl into it and I was stronger in my head than she was. A sort of heavy dependency thing came out of it which I wasn't ready for and which caused me to break off the relationship. This wasn't good for either of us. I felt really guilty. I had done the whole thing with her about caring and loving, but it really wasn't like that. It was more that I wanted to conquer her and go to bed with her. And after I had won that prize, there was no longer any motivation to care.[4]

Believing one should marry because of sexual involvement but knowing the sex partner is not right for marriage can cause agonizing mental conflict. Consider the misgivings of this college student who speaks concerning her sexual involvement with her boyfriend.

> He knows I'd rather be a virgin because when we have fights . . . I start thinking, are we still together just because we had sex. I do a lot of soul searching. I still wish I was a virgin and he wishes I was too. If we could turn the clocks back I still would be.

Pregnancy is always a possibility, and when it happens outside of marriage, it confronts a couple with painful decisions. Abortion appears to be the easy way out. I think many choose it as a means of hiding the fact of pregnancy. It's true that freeing oneself of an unwanted pregnancy can help one's social life, but many who have had an abortion pay a high emotional price. Soon after having an abortion, a twenty-two-year-old university student confessed: "I was confused and I didn't know if I wanted to get married, have the baby, or have an abortion." She added that her boyfriend pressured her to have an abortion so she did. She later regretted her hasty decision. "If I had it to do over again, I would choose to have the baby and raise it myself."[5]

Although the Supreme Court has declared abortion to be legal, it has not taken a stand on its morality. Instead of resorting to abortion to avoid the embarrassment of pregnancy, one needs to stop and think more carefully. If you decide that you and your sexual partner could not build a happy marriage, then consider continuing the pregnancy and giving the baby up for adoption. Thousands of married couples unable to have their own children want to adopt a baby but are unable to because of wholesale abortion. Eleanor and I adopted one of our five children, so we know the goodness that adoption can bring to the lives of both the parents and the child.

Another self-induced penalty resulting from nonmarital sex is sexually transmitted diseases. It is now an epidemic in our society, a major health problem. The only sure way to avoid contracting some kind of STD is to limit sexual activity to one loyal partner, and the Christian ethic teaches this should occur in marriage. Anyone who has more than one sex partner should have regular medical exams for STD diagnosis.

Even for those not morally opposed to it, potential problems can result from participation in premarital sex; therefore, I believe the practical as well as moral thing to do is to wait until marriage. However, I realize that some of you will choose the other option. Whichever you choose, remember that you are responsible for all your decisions and actions.

ON BEING RESPONSIBLE

It seems that most single persons want to avoid an unwed

pregnancy. Then why do so many people take chances? My counseling sessions with individuals and couples involved in premarital pregnancies have given me some insight. In response to the question, "Why didn't you use some kind of contraception?," I was often given the answer, "Because I didn't intend to have sex."

WHAT DO YOU INTEND TO DO?

If you plan to wait until marriage, you must act according to your decision. This means knowing how to apply emotional brakes. Self-restraint must be exercised when giving physical affection. Be honest with yourself. If you intend to comply with the Judeo-Christian code of ethics, then use the necessary self-control for the purpose of postponing sex until marriage. However, if you intend to be sexually active before marriage, medically supervised contraception should be used. This is being responsible. In many cases, failure to take personal responsibility is a reason that contraception is not used. Even though premarital pregnancy is more of a crisis for a woman than a man, it is nevertheless the man's responsibility as well as the woman's to take steps to avoid pregnancy.

In conclusion, remember that, "sex is not a commodity to be bought and sold, an isolated drive to be frustrated or satisfied and then forgotten, or simply an off-color subject to be blushed at and snickered about—but, rather, a means of saying something deep and profound about who we are in a way that both the sayer and the listener are changed."[6]

NOTES

1. J.J. Arnett, *Emerging Adulthood: the Winding Road from the Late Teens Through the Twenties* (New York: Oxford Press, 2004), 87, 89.
2. William F. May, "Four Mischievous Theories of Sex: Demonic, Divine, Casual, and Nuisance," from Willard Gaylin, MD, and Ethel Person, MD, eds., *Passionate Attachments: Thinking about Love* (New York: Free Press, 1988), 27–40. Copyright 1988 by the Friends of Columbia Psychoanalytic Center, Inc.
3. Charlie Shedd, *How to Know if You're Really in Love* (Kansas City: Shedd Andrews and McMeel, 1978), 63.
4. "About Your Sexuality," Deryck Calderwood Unitarian Universalistic Association

5.   Anonymous interview.
6.   Reverend Harry E. Smith, "Sex in Context," talk given at Florida State University.

Shopping in the Marriage Market

YOUR CHOICE OF a career and your choice of a marriage partner are two of the most important decisions you'll ever make. Your occupation will, for the most part, determine your standard of living, and the husband or wife you choose will add to or subtract from your happiness. Yet, despite the seriousness of these two decisions, many people give more thought in selecting a house or even a car than they give in selecting a marriage partner.

I used to jokingly teach that the "ABCs" of shopping for a good bargain in the marriage market were to find someone who is attractive, who is bright, and who is charming; however, there are millions of happy marriages in which neither the husband nor the wife would be described as attractive, bright, or charming. What is essential is that you find someone who is attractive to you, whose personality is appealing to you, and whose intelligence is similar to yours. It might also be exciting to marry someone who is rich and famous, but these two characteristics are luxuries we don't really need. What we do need is someone who will help us meet both our physical and our personality needs, and someone who will help us achieve our potential and develop our talents.

YOU DON'T BUY, YOU TRADE

People really do shop for marriage partners, but, unlike the marketplace of goods and services, they don't buy. They trade. No matter how intensely one may want to marry another person, a wedding of this couple will not take place unless the desire to marry is mutual. Each partner, therefore, must be willing to trade his or her qualities and quirks with those of the other. This willingness to exchange is a fundamental principle operating in the marriage market.

How do you, in a sensible way, begin to find someone who will exchange their strengths and weaknesses with yours? First, discover yourself. Determine who you are and what you are; then wholeheartedly accept what you have discovered so that you are comfortable with yourself. Compatibility with oneself is essential for a happy marriage because, otherwise, one's psychological hang-ups about himself will interfere with his ability to relate lovingly to others. In other words, you have to be happily married to yourself before you can be happily married to anyone else.

You will, furthermore, save yourself misery if you're careful to trade with someone in the marriage market who not only likes himself or herself, but also shows an unconditional, positive regard for all people. Shop for someone who dares to be tender with children, with older people, and with those who are afflicted and troubled. Look also for an individual who possesses the courage to be psychologically tough—in other words, who is assertive with others, when necessary.

WHAT SHOULD YOU LOOK FOR?

When you shop for a marriage partner, observe his concern for himself as well as his concern for others. Find someone who is health-conscious and who is doing everything possible to maintain good health because, although perfect health is not always necessary for a happy marriage, good health enhances the quality of any marriage. If you choose, for example, an individual who abuses his or her health with addictive drugs, crash diets, or improper nutrition, you may marry more trouble than you want. Is there someone else available who would be a better bargain for you? People can change bad health habits or other undesirable traits, and they sometimes do. However, you are gambling if you marry your partner before he or she makes the changes you want.

The habit of happiness, as well as good health, influences a marriage. All of us experience unfortunate incidents in life that result in temporary appropriate unhappiness. But it is important to avoid marrying someone who displays chronic unhappiness. Happiness is not a lucky accident. It is, rather, an achievement that begins with the decision to be happy despite one's circumstances, and it is accomplished through ongoing effort. Avoid committing yourself to someone who shows chronic dissatisfaction and other self-defeating patterns. Marry, instead, someone who quite consistently succeeds in school, employment, and other endeavors.

In looking for someone who is success-oriented, take care to distinguish between workaholics and easygoing winners. Some spouses are so obsessed with their careers that they are seldom home, and when they are home, they are preoccupied with their work. One of the keys to happiness is knowing how to live a balanced life. Marry someone who likes to work but also knows how to play. Every good marriage requires togetherness. Moments of togetherness, in both work and play, nurture a marriage, which takes time and effort to build and rebuild.

Partners build their marriage on the strengths they bring to it. Look carefully at your strengths and then shop for someone who decisively determines the quality of his or her life instead of just letting things happen. We determine the circumstances of our lives only when we risk making decisions and act on them. Being loyal to one's decisions denotes a mature, stable personality, while wavering back and forth after decisions are made may indicate some measure of instability. When shopping for a marriage partner, remember to look for an individual who has the ability to make decisions and accept the consequences. The single most reliable indicator of emotional maturity is the ability to make decisions and accept the consequences. We create ourselves by our choices. We determine ourselves by our decisions.

THE PEBBLE IN YOUR SHOE

Remember also that even a mature, decisive individual may, in some cases, have quirks that will irritate you. You may be able to tolerate these flaws on a three-hour date, but will you be able to tolerate the same flaws throughout a lifetime of marriage? Time-wise, dating someone is like walking across a room with that person, but marrying the individual is like walking twenty miles with him or her. Someone has compared personality quirks often found in marriage partners to a pebble in a shoe. All of us can stand the momentary unpleasantness of a pebble in a shoe if we are only walking a short distance. But if we had to walk twenty miles with that rock in our shoe, it would be a miserable experience that would result in pain and injury. What you can tolerate on a date may become intolerable in marriage. Be honest with yourself. Don't try to fool yourself into believing that love conquers all. It takes much more than love to create a satisfying marriage.

DISCOVERING REALITIES

Even though an individual's irritating traits may surface before marriage, most people are quite capable of concealing their flaws while on a date and even during courtship. Dating is play and a necessary prelude to marriage. Each couple, however, needs to work together before marriage, as well as play, in order to perceive the strengths and weaknesses within themselves and in their relationship. In your effort to discern the qualities as well as the quirks within the individual you date, keep in mind three factors: family, stress, and time.

Observing a potential marriage partner in his parent's home is important because personality quirks are more likely to emerge when he relaxes in the presence of family members. In order to observe the same individual functioning under stress, David Knox recommends that a couple skip breakfast and go on a long hike together with only enough lunch for one person. This ordeal might be stressful enough to bring out the worst in both of them. Unpleasant experiences such as the above give a couple insights into themselves and each other. If you allow yourselves sufficient time, in addition to sharing stressful experiences, you will gain a more complete and accurate picture of yourselves, both as individuals and as a couple.

TIMING

After you have given yourself the time to evaluate your dating partner and your relationship, and after you are sure that you want to marry this individual, timing becomes important. It is especially important when you must compete with others for the one you've chosen. When you know that you want to marry your dating partner and you know somebody else does also, promptly communicate your decision to your dating partner. Next, get a commitment from him or her before a promise is made to someone else.

On the other hand, don't be stampeded into a snap decision in favor of the first person who wants you. My wife and I acted promptly, but not hastily, when we realized our mutual feelings of love and the two-way competition for that love. We dated for three months before we agreed to eventually marry. After that, we had more than two years of courtship before our wedding.

SENSE APPEAL

So far in this chapter on mate selection, we have considered the personalities and the behavior of both dating partners and the necessity of evaluating the relationship itself. Now let us consider that which probably first attracted you to your dating partner— his or her physical appearance. It is important for you to marry someone who is physically attractive and sexually appealing to you because, through the years of marriage, you will find it easier to respond favorably to such a mate.

You have probably known of persons who ended a romantic relationship because they lost the feeling of attraction for the partner. You may also know of persons whose romance never gained momentum because "the chemistry wasn't right." You perceive the totality of another person through the use of your five senses. To quite an extent, your sense perceptions will influence your decision to marry or not to marry a certain dating partner. You might discover that although you perceive your partner to be healthy, attractive, and clean, you nevertheless feel slightly "allergic" to this person's biochemistry. Trust your senses and take this seriously because, for ongoing feelings of romance, the chemistry has got to be right.

He or She Is OK, but Maybe Not for You

In addition to marrying someone who has most of the qualities you want, you need to marry someone with whom you are well matched; that is, marry someone whose lifestyle and life goals are compatible with yours. Your lifestyle is the way you live your life day in and day out. Your life goals are what you want to accomplish during your lifetime. Without compatibility in these areas, a marriage is likely to break down. For example, in the old classic movie *The Way We Were,* Barbra Streisand and Robert Redford are portrayed as a couple in love. Their lifestyles and life goals were so divergent that a lifetime of happiness would have been virtually impossible. Therefore, they ended their relationship.

Compatible personalities, as well as compatible lifestyles and life goals, are necessary for a happy marriage. Personalities, although different, may yet be compatible if there is a good psychological fit between a couple. Compatible personalities, moreover, give a couple the potential to develop the kind of relationship described by Anne Morrow Lindbergh in *Gift from the Sea:*

> A good relationship has a pattern like a dance and is built on some of the same rules. The partners do not need to hold on tightly, because they move confidently in the same pattern, intricate but gay and swift and free like a country dance of Mozart's. There is no place here for the possessive clutch, the clinging arm, the heavy hand; only the barest touch in passing. Now, arm in arm, now face to face, now back to back—it does not matter which. Because they know they are partners moving in the same rhythm, creating a pattern together, and being invisibly nourished by it.[1]

The above passage shows that a couple, who find it easy to be very close, can also be willing to grant each other the freedom to be separate, distinct individuals.

Where Should You Shop?

Dating, or at least relating closely to many persons of the other sex, adds to your chances of finding someone who will give you the freedom to be yourself, who has the qualities you want, and whose lifestyle, life goals, and personality are compatible with your own.

Having many heterosexual friendships gives you a broad basis for comparison and, therefore, selection.

Where should one shop for this suitable, compatible mate? First of all, keep in mind that most people date and eventually marry someone near their own residence, or they meet someone in the same educational or employment locations. Among these people, try to associate especially with those persons who you perceive would share your values and interests. For example, affiliate with certain campus, civic, and church organizations. There are many of them to choose from.

If you are attending a college or university, join a club that pertains to your chosen field of study. Likewise, join a civic organization centered around your special interest. If marrying within your faith is important to you, join a church club such as a Roman Catholic Newman Club or a Latter-day Saints Student Association, both of which are located on college and university campuses across the nation. If there are a very small number of students of your own faith at your local campus, you will strengthen the probability that you will marry within your religion if you attend a church school such as Northwest Nazarene University, Notre Dame, or Brigham Young University. If it is important to you to marry someone who has a farm or ranch background, it might be a good idea for you to study or work in a rural setting. Know yourself well enough to be able to decide what you want and need in a marriage partner.

As you shop in any one of the marriage markets, remember that among the billions of people in the world, there are hundreds—and possibly thousands—of different people with whom you could be happily married. On the other hand, there are just as many individuals with whom you could be miserably married. Shop carefully in the market of love because your choice of a marriage partner may be the most important decision you will ever make.

NOTE

1. Anne Morrow Lindbergh, *Gift from the Sea* (New York: Random House, 2003), 151–52.

5

Should You Marry Your Fiancé?

YOUR ENGAGEMENT IS an agreement—a promise to marry a certain person. The beginning of your engagement is probably a joyous time for both you and your fiancé because you have each won the heart and commitment of the other. You have become engaged because it appears to you that your love is strong enough and you are well enough matched to spend a happy lifetime together.

WHY BE ENGAGED?

The major functions of the engagement, according to Jerome Folkman and Nancy Clatworthy, are: "(1) To give the individuals an opportunity to know each other in a situation of commitment where competitors and the false 'line' are less likely to be presented; (2) To help the couple feel the 'ties' and 'push' of social pressure; (3) To pair them socially and psychologically; and (4) To have them become better acquainted with each other's family, friends, and social patterns."[1]

A secret engagement is contradictory. It does not serve one of the purposes of engagement, which is to give notice to others who may be interested in this woman or man that they are out of circulation, that they are no longer available. A public engagement also informs family members and friends of your serious intent to marry. This will probably generate some feedback to you which may be beneficial in finalizing your decision to be or not to be married to your fiancé.

Time to say good-bye to the past and develop new habits: Are there activities and personal habits that will be forever altered because of your marriage? Perhaps you go out with your work friends every Friday evening. Or maybe you have a personal habit you know will have to change when your spouse moves in—you leave your dirty clothes lying on the bedroom floor, or you take up all the bathroom counter space with your cosmetics. Have you been living with your best friend from college for the last five years? Leaving that situation may, in some ways, be as momentous as moving in with your new spouse. You'll need to grieve the loss of that familiarity and friendship as you celebrate finding your soul mate and cherished love in your spouse. . . .

. . . Take charge of the process and put closure on your past now, when you have the time and ability to say good-bye in your own way. After you are married you may be so consumed with building your new life that you may resent the sudden changes in habit you hadn't prepared for. . . .

. . . Certainly planning a wedding and preparing for a marriage will give you numerous opportunities to work together, to surmount obstacles, and to endure stress. Your ability to pull together instead of to push apart will be tested daily. While this process may be stressful, it can be beneficial to your future life together.[2]

Your engagement means that you have made a tentative decision to marry a certain person. An engagement may be broken, but while it lasts, it should signify what might be called an emotional and moral commitment; otherwise it becomes meaningless. There should be no doubt in the minds of the man and woman that the other is his or her final choice of a marriage partner. If there is a doubt, there should be no engagement.

How Long Should You Be Engaged?

Your engagement must be long enough for both you and your fiancé to be convinced that your relationship has high potential for success or for at least one of you to conclude that it lacks this potential. You might be able to determine this in a few months, or it may take you a year or longer. The longer you are engaged to your fiancé, the more you will learn about each other and about your relationship. If you break up, it can be assumed that you, your fiancé, or maybe both of you, decided that your relationship was inadequate for a lifetime together. If you choose to marry after an engagement of a reasonable length of time, it can be assumed that you were satisfied with the new information that you acquired during your engagement.

The intensity and quality of a relationship are more important than the length of engagement time. If Kevin and Heidi are engaged for two years and she spends the first year of that time studying in Paris and he spends the second year of their engagement overseas in the military service, their engagement relationship has not been adequate for them to know for sure that they are right for each other. Being together during engagement as often as possible is necessary so that you can accurately evaluate each other and your relationship. I am acquainted with a couple who had a six-year courtship and with another couple who had only a five-month engagement. Both couples appear to be very happily married. The length of your engagement is less important than what you accomplish during that engagement.

CAN AN ENGAGEMENT BE TOO LONG?

If engagement is a transition, it should not last indefinitely. Couples should not get engaged until they know when the wedding will be (what month or at least what season). To be engaged with no end in sight is too stagnant. Engagement is not an end in itself but a commitment to get married. Its meaning is distorted unless the goal is calendared.

A love relationship naturally gains in momentum as it progresses from the first meeting to mutual love to an engagement commitment to the wedding and honeymoon. Love can be a "many-splendored thing," but if a couple is repeatedly frustrated and diverted from their marriage goal by military service or schooling and career obligations, their relationship may lose its vitality. It is unrealistic, I think, for you to expect to complete all your career preparations prior to your marriage. My wife and I had a courtship of nearly three years. After our wedding, I attended college for three more years, and for nearly three years I worked as a salesman before going to Florida State University to work on my doctorate degree. Had we postponed marriage until I had completed all my education and career preparations, our courtship would have been about ten years in duration, and I don't think our case is unusual.

I do not wish to give you the impression that I think you should marry immediately after falling in love, for under a number of circumstances it is wise to postpone marriage. If you are in the military with an assignment overseas where your husband or wife could not accompany you, you may be wise to postpone your wedding. I say this because a long separation immediately after a wedding would likely be disappointing to both of you and a poor situation for beginning a lifetime of marriage. Postponing the wedding until after you are reunited may be desirable.

REVEALING YOURSELF

Maybe you are bothered about some event in your family history or some personal activity in which you have engaged. Should you inform your fiancé?

In wondering what to confess to your fiancé, if anything, take into account the following considerations: (1) Do I have a legal obligation to tell? (2) Even though I am not legally bound to confess this, do I feel a moral obligation to do so? (3) Is it highly likely that my fiancé will find out from someone else? (4) Is my fiancé the kind of person who desires to know everything about my background and personal history? (5) Will revealing this information help or hurt our relationship?

Reflecting on what to confess to a fiancé, Bowman advises:

> By and large it is better to let the other person volunteer information, and to accept what he volunteers as the whole truth, than it is to pry through curiosity into experiences which the other person has long ago buried. . . . No one is under obligation to bring all of the skeletons out of the closet just because he or she has become engaged. It is only fair play, however, to reveal anything that has bearing on the couple's future relationship. . . . Whatever is revealed should be told before the wedding. If it is told after the wedding, the other person may feel trapped.[3]

29

A fiancé is entitled to know any of the following facts about a partner: That he or she has been married, is a parent, is sterile, has a serious hereditary defect or a life-threatening health condition, or has a prison record. After learning of these negative circumstances about you, your fiancé may want to break the engagement. However, it is to the advantage of both of you that these kinds of circumstances be revealed before marriage rather than after. You take a risk when you confess something negative about yourself to your intended marriage partner, but you may be taking a greater risk by not confessing. It is far better for both of you that you undergo a broken engagement rather than a divorce.

Separation during Engagement

Let's suppose that you and your partner are sure that you want to marry but you soon must be separated for a long time, a year or longer. Under these circumstances, you may be better off to be engaged informally. When a man and woman have agreed to marry but are not ready to formalize their engagement with a ring and an announcement, they have an informal engagement.

If your partner chooses to date during the time you are apart, this may increase the likelihood that he or she will remain true to you. Prior to your separation, if you insist on a formal engagement and thus deny your partner the freedom to date, you may increase your risk of breaking up. Your fiancé may become tired of a dull, uneventful social life and may finally break the engagement in order to have freedom to date. One study found that more college women who were dating others while separated from their fiancé-to-be kept their promise to marry than those who did no dating.[4]

It was concluded that an agreement never to date while separated from one's fiancé may be too binding and frustrating and may contribute to a broken engagement. My wife and I were separated during the second year of our three-year courtship. We had agreed to marry, but she chose not to accept an engagement ring because she wanted to date while I was gone. I accepted this with some anxiety. But after our reunion, I was assured that the more she had dated, the more convinced she became that we were well suited for each other.

COMMUNICATING WHILE APART

During a long time apart, it is important for the two of you to communicate often in a variety of ways. This is necessary in order for you to be aware of changes in your partner and to keep your relationship growing. Send letters and photos, do email and texting, and make phone calls. If you remain true to each other throughout the time of your separation, you would be wise to give yourselves time to reevaluate each other and your relationship following your reunion before making definite wedding arrangements.

A CAREFUL LOOK AT YOURSELF AND YOUR FIANCÉ

Are you ready for marriage? Is your partner ready for marriage? Are the two of you compatible? Stop and look carefully at yourself and your partner.

1. Are you both success-oriented? A person is successful if he sets goals and works toward them. He is unsuccessful, no matter how hard he may be working, if he has no goals in mind.
2. Are you both health-oriented? Do you do everything possible to maintain and enhance your physical and mental health?
3. Are you and your partner happiness-oriented? Lincoln said that people are about as happy as they make up their minds to be. Though spoken centuries ago, the wisdom of King Solomon can be applied today to improve health and happiness: "A cheerful heart is a good medicine."[5]
4. What kind of marriage do your fiancé's parents have? For about twenty years this has been your fiancé's marriage model. Your partner's marriage ability will be helped or hindered by the kind of marriage he or she has grown up with.

Each of you may think the other is wonderful. It's all right to have stars in your eyes, but be careful not to have rocks in your head. You and your fiancé will find it easy to be pleasant when the two of you are sharing fun activities; however, marriage involves work as well as play. How pleasant is your fiancé when working? It is important to see and evaluate your partner's personality while at work. If you go to the Friday-night ball game together, on Saturday don't just play more but go to the library and study together. Then add hunger and decision-making to your relationship by skipping lunch and going shopping. This should bring out at least some of the worst in both of you. Are you both still sure that you want to spend over a half century together? Work together as well as play. Worship together if you are both religiously inclined. Meet and interact as often as possible with your fiancé's family members and friends. Getting to know them is an important part of getting to know your intended marriage partner better.

Be sure your fiancé is going in life where you want to go. What are his or her major life goals? To learn more about this, you could exchange written statements of what your goals are.

Beware of Danger Signs

If one or more of the following danger signs develop in your relationship, you should seriously consider breaking your engagement:

1. *Conflicting lifestyles.* A person's interests and values largely determine his style of life. Suppose that Roy and Andrea are engaged. Roy's interests and style of life center around farming and ranching. There is nothing he'd rather do than drive a tractor with a plow cutting the soil behind or ride a horse with a herd of cattle ahead. Andrea's interests and lifestyle are very different from Roy's. She grew up in Los Angeles, with the hustle and bustle of city life. She thinks farming is dirty drudgery and ranching is lonely boredom. With such different interests and lifestyles, Roy and Andrea are poorly suited for each other, though they could be excellent marriage partners for someone else.

   Suppose your style of life is characterized by reading, listening to music, and socializing with a limited number of friends. Your fiancé's lifestyle is one of restless activity. He often visits night spots and seems to have a constant influx of friends and acquaintances. With such drastically

different lifestyles, you may be performing an act of kindness for your fiancé as well as yourself by breaking your
engagement.

2. *Different values and life goals.* A person's values determine his
    life goals. Consider this couple: Russell values Bible reading,
    church attendance, and service to others. His career goal is
    to become a minister, and he is engaged to marry Denise,
    who places little value on religion and has grown up in an
    affluent home. She values a life of luxury and leisure, and her
    goal is to have a lot of money someday. With such different
    values and life goals, Russell and Denise should probably
    break their engagement. Remember, being in love is not
    enough for a happy marriage.

    A few years ago, a college girl came into my office to
    confer with me about her engagement. She was troubled
    because her fiancé wanted children but she did not and had
    not told him. Their wedding date was only a month away.
    This is an example of a crucial difference in personal values
    and life goals, enough of a difference to warrant breaking
    an engagement.

3. *Personality clash.* In his song, "Raindrops Keep Falling on
    My Head," Burt Bacharach says, "nothing seems to fit." This
    describes the way it is for a couple that does not have a good
    personality blend. They are emotionally and psychologically
    incompatible. If your future marriage is to survive, the two
    of you must have a good personality fit—like a glove that fits
    a hand. Compatibility means you feel comfortable together
    and find it easy to be yourself and let your fiancé be himself
    or herself. It means that most of the time you are on the same
    wavelength. If you are compatible, your relationship "clicks."
    The most reliable indicator of interpersonal compatibility
    is the amount of enjoyment and satisfaction that each of
    you derive from the company of the other. The importance
    of a couple's happiness when they are together cannot be
    overemphasized.

4. *A desire to remodel your partner.* Another courtship danger

sign is a strong desire to change many things about your partner. In most human relationships, there are certain behavioral traits that each has that are slightly annoying to the other. Some of these can be tolerated, and some can be changed. But if you become aware that you are often annoyed about many of your partner's traits and can hardly wait until after your wedding so you can launch into a project of "partner overhaul," forget it. Break your engagement and look for someone who more completely fulfills your image of the ideal mate.

5. *Loss of interest:* Loss of interest should be taken seriously, for if a couple cannot maintain interest in each other in the rather casual and playful relationships of engagement, how long could their interest survive in marriage?

I know of a woman who broke her engagement six days before her wedding date. If you have not yet gone through your wedding ceremony, it is not too late to break your engagement. If it is clear to you that you should not marry your fiancé, don't hesitate to break your engagement because of overconcern about what people will think. Even if you have sent out invitations and made last-minute wedding arrangements, have the courage to break your engagement if you think you should do so.

One or both of you may become increasingly disappointed and disenchanted with the other. You may become more and more aware of tension, unpleasantness, and conflicting values between you. One of you may say, "Maybe we shouldn't spend so much time together," or "Maybe we should break up." If your partner clearly communicates a wish to break the engagement, you might respond with a relieved, "Yes, I think so too." But if you oppose the breakup, your response will be quite different.

If you have decided to break your engagement, do not allow yourself to be dissuaded by drastic threats made by your fiancé. Outlandish threats to drop out of school, quit one's job, go on drugs, or commit suicide are seldom carried out; but when they are, one is not responsible for the fiancé's behavior. You must not allow yourself to be pressured into an unwise marriage because of threats being made by your fiancé.

Adjusting to a Broken Engagement

Serious loss of any kind usually results in depression. One who has lost a lover is in a state of bereavement. Bereavement means "to take away from" and is a form of emotional illness related to loss, but it need not be lengthy or permanent. A few months ago, I counseled by phone and by letter with a young university woman whose boyfriend broke up with her. Her despondency and general emotional illness induced by this event was brief because she expanded her interest to others and launched into new adventurous activities.

You may have accumulated sentimental tokens that symbolize the love between you and your fiancé. These could include gifts you have exchanged, letters, photographs, and recordings. Don't torture yourself by repeatedly looking at them and reminiscing about your bygone relationship. Don't allow yourself to think that you will never again win the heart of another with qualities equal to those of your lost love. Don't indoctrinate yourself with the thought that your former fiancé was your "one and only" and the most wonderful person who could ever be for you. Stop thinking about what you have lost! When your thoughts drift to what is no longer yours, say to yourself, "Stop it!" Make the most of what you have and the least of what you do not have.

Be slow to commit yourself to a new partner after breaking your engagement. You might try to cope with your loss by trying to quickly replace your fiancé with someone else. This tendency is shown by how quickly many people remarry after divorce. When you are ready to date again, go out with as many individuals as possible to give you a broad basis for comparison.

Engagement Counseling

There may be enough danger signs in your relationship so that you are seriously considering breaking your engagement. A capable marriage and family therapist may be of considerable help to you in making the important decision to marry or not to marry your fiancé.

Or perhaps you are not contemplating breaking your engagement, but your relationship has problems that a marriage counselor could help you overcome. You might benefit from engagement counseling even though you are sure you want to marry your fiancé and have no major conflicts in your relationship. A professional marriage therapist can give you valuable information, such as names of reliable books on love, sex, marriage, and parenthood. He can also raise important questions for you and your fiancé to consider. A talk with a marriage counselor can add to your confidence and optimism.

There are premarriage questionnaires to help a couple evaluate areas where they may have challenges in adjustment or problems in their future marriage. An example is "Relate" and other relationship assessments available online.[6]

Part of your engagement counseling should be with a medical doctor for a thorough physical examination. I think it would be wise for both of you to have a physical exam shortly before your intended wedding date so that you may know the state of your health. In case your doctor discovers any serious health condition, it would only be fair for you to reveal this information to your fiancé. Also, a careful exam can give you, as a couple, assurance that sexual love will be possible without complications, and at this time, you will probably want to consult with the physician about methods of contraception.

CAN YOU AND YOUR FIANCÉ HAVE A SATISFYING MARRIAGE?

You probably can . . .

1. *If you have compatible lifestyles, life goals, and personalities.*
2. *If you have knowledge about marriage.* You are willing to study and prepare for your career because you want to succeed at it. Likewise, isn't it reasonable that you are more likely to succeed at marriage if you are educated for it? You and your fiancé are more likely to have a satisfying marriage if you are willing to learn and keep learning.
3. *If you both have skill.* Knowledge alone is of little value unless

one can apply it. Skills at the art of living and in human relations enhance one's marriageability. This requires that we reduce our self-centeredness. The more mature one is, the less self-centered he is. The spouse who is completely wrapped up in himself is incapable of sustaining a profoundly affectionate relationship. The completely self-centered person is incapable of love. One who is all wrapped up in himself makes a small package.

4. *If you both make an ongoing effort to have a good marriage.* You may have compatibility, knowledge, and skill and yet have an unsatisfying marriage unless you both make a strong effort to have a good marriage. Many couples stay married with little satisfaction, with little joy in the relationship. These marriages are devitalized. They are like a flat tire or a dying fire. Because of carelessness and a lack of effort, the flames of marriage have dwindled to smoldering coals. The effort made by both partners to have a good marriage can make the difference between excellence and mediocrity.

5. *If you have the support of friends and relatives.* This will make you and your fiancé more likely to have a happy marriage. The extent to which your friends and relatives approve or disapprove of your relationship can influence your marital success. At times of trouble in your marriage, emotional support from key individuals in your lives can give you the lift you need to stay together. The opposite is also true. If people important to both of you think your marriage was a mistake and that you ought to end it, this may convince you to call it quits.

6. *If you are both willing to make a wholehearted commitment.* You'd better look around for another partner if you are so unsure about your fiancé that you cannot think of yourself being married to your fiancé for a lifetime. Marriage partners handicap their union unless they are committed to it wholeheartedly and without reservation. The lack of commitment on the part of either or both of the pair deprives them of the cohesiveness needed to sustain the marriage.

Do You and Your Fiancé Agree on Most Things?

The more you and your partner are in agreement, the more you will enjoy each other and the fewer arguments you will have. It's very important that you find someone to marry with whom you more often agree than disagree.

For a more careful evaluation of whether you should marry your fiancé, a website based on research is available at https://www.relate-institute.org.

Notes

1. Jerome D. Folkman and Clatworthy, Nancy, M. K., *Marriage Has Many Faces* (Columbus, Ohio: Merrill, 1970), 77.

2. David and Claudia Arp, "Secrets of a Great Engagement," chapter 2 in Les Parrott III and Leslie Parrot, eds. *Getting Ready for the Wedding: All You Need to Know before You Say I Do*, (Michigan: Zondervan, 1998), 31–32, 37. Used by permission.

3. Henry A. Bowman, Marriage for Moderns, 5th edition (New York: McGraw-Hill, 1965).

4. From the master's thesis of William Rolfe Kerr, "Implication of Absentee Courtship," available from the Utah State University Library, Logan, Utah.

5. Proverbs 17:22, Revised Standard Version.

6. "Relate" can be found at www.relate-institute.org.

PART II

Shifting Gears in Your Marriage

For happy marriages and satisfying relationships, family members need knowledge and skill in human relations. Final adjustment in marriage and the family is never fully achieved. It is a process that involves ongoing changes by all members of a happy family. The art of relating and adjusting to others is the theme of part two.

Most marriages don't need a major overhaul; they just need a minor tune-up from time to time. And this is true of all relationships. Guiding you and your loved ones in tuning up your relationships is a major goal of this book, especially part two.

Happy couples have learned how to communicate better, not necessarily more. Communicating more negatives can hurt the quality of a marriage. Complaining, criticizing, and contending are communications that corrode relationships.

In part two, you can also read why anger more often hurts than helps relationships and why sexual love is an important dimension of a happy marriage.

Your Interpersonal
Competence for Marriage

A COUPLE CAN have a happy marriage even though they have a considerable number of differences, such as nationality, age, educational levels, and socioeconomic status, provided they have basically the same values and both have ability in human relations—interpersonal competence. Having essentially the same values is important because our values determine our choice of a lifestyle and life goals. The more differences between a husband and wife, the more adjustments they'll have to make, but they will have many adjustments even when they have few differences. Adjusting and readjusting in close relationships requires skill in human relations. How do you perceive yourself in this manner?

Evaluate your abilities as a marriage partner by checking a number one through five, five indicating the best level.

ABILITIES AS A MARRIAGE PARTNER

For Yourself	1	2	3	4	5
Ability to control your anger					
Ability to harmlessly communicate your anger					

For Yourself	1	2	3	4	5
Ability to say "good-bye" in such a way that it leaves a pleasant memory for the day					
Effort to express enthusiasm when seeing and greeting your partner					
Ability to speak clearly and understandably					
Ability to listen and comprehend					
Effort to use a pleasant tone of voice					
Frequency of expressing affection					
Frequency of expressing appreciation					
Tendency to yield to your partner's wishes					
Effort to learn about your mate's work, interests, and activities					
Contribution to the financial security of your marriage and family					
Effort to be an appealing and satisfying sexual partner					
Effort to be an informed, capable parent					
Inclination to apologize when you have offended someone					
Readiness to forgive after someone has wronged you					

For Yourself	1	2	3	4	5
Effort to develop a sense of humor about your marriage, circumstances, and especially yourself					
To what extent do you believe that you and your partner are emotionally bonded to each other?					
For Your Partner	1	2	3	4	5
Ability to control your anger					
Ability to harmlessly communicate your anger					
Ability to say "good-bye" in such a way that it leaves a pleasant memory for the day					
Effort to express enthusiasm when seeing and greeting your partner					
Ability to speak clearly and understandably					
Ability to listen and comprehend					
Effort to use a pleasant tone of voice					
Frequency of expressing affection					
Frequency of expressing appreciation					
Tendency to yield to your partner's wishes					

For Your Partner	1	2	3	4	5
Effort to learn about your mate's work, interests, and activities					
Contribution to the financial security of your marriage and family					
Effort to be an appealing and satisfying sexual partner					
Effort to be an informed, capable parent					
Inclination to apologize when you have offended someone					
Readiness to forgive after someone has wronged you					
Effort to develop a sense of humor about your marriage, circumstances, and especially yourself					
To what extent do you believe that you and your partner are emotionally bonded to each other?					

It is recommended that you respond to each item of your partner's self-appraisal by saying to what extent you agree. If you wish, you may use the terms "agree," "strongly agree," "disagree," or "strongly disagree."

Adjustment in
Marriage Means Change

HUSBANDS AND WIVES are less likely to believe they've married beneath themselves or to consider poisoning brandy if they know how to adjust. From my experience as a husband and marriage counselor, I have concluded that couples who have an enjoyable marriage know how to consistently adjust and readjust in at least five ways. To help you remember these, I call them *the five C's of change* in marriage adjustment. They are *capitulating, convincing, compromising, changing certain undesirable circumstances,* and a *change in attitude about something.*

Marriage adjustment means changes in yourself, in your partner, in unwanted circumstances, and in your mind. A couple must often make changes and adjustments if a marriage is to mature and grow. But for newlyweds, so many changes need to be made at once that adjustment is especially difficult.

CAPITULATING—MAKING CERTAIN ONGOING CHANGES IN YOURSELF

1. I Change First

Each of us needs to make a decision to change first. When one person improves in a relationship, the other one usually does also.

However, if both partners choose to wait for the other to change before making personal improvements, holy wedlock will remain in a state of unholy deadlock.

If you are to save your marriage and enrich its quality, you might need to change your attitude about your marriage partner. An attitude is merely a way of thinking about someone or something. You might even need to experience a mighty change in your heart. You may also need to change certain actions—that is, how you treat your partner. Love is as love does. Our actions include our manner of speaking.

A willingness to make certain ongoing changes in yourself to please your partner is the first important aspect of marriage adjustment. It has been said that wives have many faults, but the greatest of all is, "They please themselves too often and their husbands too seldom." I think husbands have many faults also, and the greatest of all is, "They please themselves too often and their wives too seldom." In happy marriages, both husband and wife make a continual effort to try to please each other.

A. Expectations—Before you can please your marriage partner, you have to know what he or she expects of you. Does your husband expect you to get up and prepare his breakfast for him? Does your wife want you to be home by a certain time in the evening? If you don't know what your mate expects of you, find out so you can try to meet these expectations.

B. Radar—To please your partner more, imagine that you have a built-in radar screen for picking up signals. This screen can show you what's bothering your mate about your behavior. Then, for a better marriage, do more of what your partner likes and less of what he or she dislikes.

C. Responding to Feedback—Too much talking on the telephone or leaving your coat lying around may be upsetting to your mate. Your radar may pick up only a sigh, a frown, or an outright complaint. However the feedback comes, accept it and consider changing yourself to please your partner. Your spouse's reactions should not be taken as criticism. These responses can be an avenue to self-improvement.

When we are criticized, we tend to counterattack with a complaint of our own. This can trigger an argument, causing us to forget the original message. When your partner complains, instead of reversing the charges, fix in your mind what changes he or she wants you to make. Try writing yourself reminder notes of what your partner would like you to start doing or stop doing. Making changes is part of a growing marriage.

D. Yielding to Your Partner's Wishes—I've usually been willing to submit myself to my wife's wishes. I can think of only three situations in which I would not yield to her. If she wanted me to do something that (1) is illegal, (2) is immoral, or (3) would violate my basic personality, such as to never again listen to country music. Anything else that Eleanor might want me to do, I am willing to do in order to please her and enhance our relationship.

For a satisfying love relationship, you too will need to make certain changes according to your mate's wishes. However, if you are well matched as a couple, neither one of you will have to change your basic personality to please the other—you will just need to change your manner of relating to one another from time to time. Whenever you yield to the wishes of your partner, it is important that it be done as an act of love. Giving in with cooperative kindness can elevate your self-esteem as well as elicit a positive response. Acquiescing with resentment, on the other hand, doesn't help either of you feel good.

2. Convincing Your Partner to Make Certain Changes

If your husband or wife occasionally leaves clothes lying around the bedroom or neglects to replace the toothpaste cap, this may not bother you. But if this goes on day after day, 365 days a year, it may become very annoying to you. "A minor habit may assume the proportions of a weakness of character," writes Ray E. Baber in *Marriage and the Family.* If you're irritated by something like this, tell your mate because the second important part of marriage adjustment is convincing our partners to make certain ongoing changes.

A. The Art of Persuasion—While I was a student in Tallahassee, Florida, we owned a portable typewriter. Eleanor said she wanted to sell it and buy an upright. I liked our small typewriter, so I resisted the idea. Ellie was smart enough not to try to nag me into her way of thinking. Instead, she had an upright typewriter delivered to our house on a tryout basis. I reminded her that I was not giving up our portable. She said, "Okay, but just try it out and see how you like it." After a few days, she noticed I was using the new one more often than the old one. Then with good timing and persuasion, she convinced me that we should sell the old one and buy the new one. In like manner, we have evolved to the use of computers, email, and so on.

B. Nagging Won't Help—Tell your partner what changes you want, but *do not nag*! The dictionary says nagging is "repeatedly urging, scolding, and faultfinding." Not only do some wives nag, but so do some husbands. A person who is nagged soon learns to tune out. Nagging does not motivate a person to change, and it may result in a loss of goodwill.

How can we motivate someone to change his or her behavior without nagging?

First, we must keep in mind what nagging is. It is *repeatedly* urging, scolding, and faultfinding. Then we need to think of what we can do to get our partner to change without nagging.

Let's suppose your husband habitually leaves his slippers lying around on the bedroom floor. Tell him that you would like him to put them in the closet. Try to get a commitment from him. Then, be patient and pleasant instead of nagging him if he leaves his slippers out from time to time. Remind him in a good-natured way. Use your imagination about how you can get him to correct his habit. If you know he is going golfing, you might hang his neglected slippers on his golf clubs. Whatever you do, make it fun for both of you. We are more likely to succeed in motivating a person to do something if we can show him that he has something to gain from it.

C. Timing Is Important—In trying to convince your mate to do something or not to do something, use good timing. Suppose a husband has been thinking he ought to talk with his wife about their overdrawn checking account. He is not using good timing if he brings up the subject as soon as he arrives home from work. At this time, he doesn't know what kind of a day she's had or what kind of a mood she's in—possibly she isn't feeling well. If she's had a bad day, she may respond with defensiveness and anger. Because we are usually hungry at this time of day and more likely to respond unkindly and irrationally, it is not a good time to bring up a point of criticism.

Complaining at bedtime is also poor timing. Suppose a wife has been thinking that for several days her husband has put off mowing the lawn. It's 11:30 at night. They're lying together in bed. He's dropping off to sleep, and she says to him, "George, what about the lawn?" He mumbles, "What lawn?" She replies, "Our lawn! It's not cut yet." Then he speaks with anger because he is tired. But she is upset with him for procrastinating, so she also responds with anger. You can imagine the rest—an argument, resulting in hurt feelings and loss of sleep.

The marriage bed is for two things—sleeping and making love. It is not for criticizing nor for discussing points of difference.

3. Compromising

Suppose that Bill and Susan are newlyweds and disagree about their Saturday night recreation. Bill enjoys bowling and would like Susan to go with him, but she prefers the movies and would like his company. What can they do to adjust? Each can try to persuade the other to accept his or her form of recreation. If one wins the other over, this is good. If neither succeeds in convincing the other, maybe they can compromise. One Saturday night they can go to the movies and the next they can go bowling. If neither will yield, they must agree to disagree.

Agreeing to disagree is a form of adjustment. Once they have agreed on a mutually satisfactory solution, neither should continue trying to convince the other to change. They need to be tolerant enough to accept this as a difference between them and let it go at that. Compromising can also include a process of bargaining such as a concession to do something for the partner, provided he or she will do something for you. Doing this is called quid pro quo, which means something for something.

4. Changing Undesirable Circumstances

Willingness to make changes within yourself and knowing how to get your partner to make changes can improve your marriage. But what do you do when you reach an impasse, when neither of you is willing to change? In this case, try changing the circumstances.

I remember when my wife and I disagreed about how firm we wanted the mattress on our bed. It all started when Eleanor began waking up with backaches and decided that a firmer mattress would prevent them. To fix the situation, we got a big sheet of plywood and put it between the mattress and the box springs. Then I began waking up with back pain. "This board has got to go," I said. "No, it's staying here," she said. Two things were clear: I wasn't going to change and neither was she. What did we do? We used a power saw and cut the board right down the middle. Now Eleanor is sleeping firm and I'm sleeping soft. This time we adjusted—not by changing ourselves nor by persuading each other to change, but by changing the situation. Simple circumstance changes can greatly improve relationships. Buying "sock sorters" for every member of the family prevents socks from getting lost and avoids having to mate them. Putting a lock on the bedroom door can help couples add spontaneity and other qualities to their sexual relationship.

5. Cognitive Changes

Cognition has to do with thoughts and attitudes. You can often increase your level of satisfaction by simply changing your mind about some undesirable situation that cannot be changed. For example, you may wish that your husband had more money and more hair or that your wife was more slim and better educated. Marriage adjustment means change, but your partner cannot change some things and will not change other things. When it is clear to you that your mate cannot or will not change something, accept it. Change your mind instead, and accept the unchangeable.

Reframing is relabeling behavior to help change how marriage partners and other family members respond to it.

If you have a painting and you decide to change the frame, this painting will look somewhat different because you have reframed it.

Likewise you can improve your attitude toward a marriage partner or anyone by reframing in your mind certain aspects of that person's behavior.

For example, if your marriage partner is ambitious and puts in long hours at his or her career, you might be inclined to complain that you are married to a "workaholic." However, what is an underlying positive is that your partner is more likely to be successful, and you as a family will have a higher income.

If your husband or wife is more romantic than you and has a stronger sexual desire, you might regard this to be a nuisance to you, but there is an underlying positive. You are lucky that your partner finds you to be attractive and sexually appealing. Because of this, you as a couple will more often have romantic and sexual experiences together. This will help you frequently renew and revitalize your love for each other.

In her book *Light Her Fire*, Dr. Ellen Kreidman gives the following examples of psychological relational reframes:

Negative—She talks too much. *Positive*—She's so friendly and puts everyone at ease.

Negative—She argues so much. *Positive*—She has such strong convictions

Negative—She's so conceited. *Positive*—She has so much confidence in herself.

Negative—She's too easygoing *Positive*—She really has a calming effect on everyone.

Negative—She's so stingy. *Positive*—She's trying to save money for our future.

Negative—She spends too much money. *Positive*—She's always trying to improve our lifestyle.

Negative—She's too rigid. *Positive*—She's really very organized.

Negative—She thinks she knows it all. *Positive*—She really is quite intelligent.

Negative—She can never sit still. *Positive*—She has so much energy.[1]

You are encouraged to make up your own reframes relevant to

certain tendencies of your partner or anyone with whom you are closely associated.

"If one doesn't understand, admire, respect and at times forgive the nuances of the opposite sex, then the beauty and satisfaction that can arise from the uniting of man and woman in the most important covenant of marriage will not be discovered and enjoyed."[2]

In summary, the 5 C's of change in marriage, or in any close relationship, are (1) capitulating to the wishes of the other person, (2) convincing and motivating the other individual to make changes, (3) compromising, in which each meets the other in the middle concerning a certain difference between them, (4) changing undesirable circumstances, and (5) changing one's attitude about certain aspects of the relationship that cannot be changed.

Husbands and wives in satisfying marriages realize that adjustment is a never-ending process. It requires a continual effort to bring about changes in yourself, in your partner, in unwanted circumstances, and in your mind. Every human being must continue to readjust himself to other people. We come up short in human relations if we fail to improve.

AREAS OF CHANGE QUESTIONNAIRE

In every relationship there are behaviors about which one or both partners seek change. These particular behaviors may occur too often or too frequently. For example, a partner may be dissatisfied because the other only takes out the garbage once a week. The change wanted would be that the behavior occurs *more often*. On the other hand, one might be dissatisfied because he thought too much time was spent cleaning up the house. In this case the change wanted would be that this behavior occurs *less often*.

The following areas of behavior have to do with relationships— their being strengthened or weakened by the quantity or quality of behavior occurring. As you read each item, decide whether you are satisfied with the performance of your spouse. Indicate the direction of change you would like—either more or less of that particular behavior. Please place your initials by all requested changes that you agree to make.

ITEMS FOR YOURSELF

I Would Like My Partner To:	Satisfied	Less	More	Major Item
Manage money wisely				
Spend time keeping the house clean				
Have meals ready on time				
Pay attention to grooming and appearance				
Get together with friends				
Prepare interesting meals				
Show appreciation for things I do				
Get together with my relatives				
Have sexual relations with me				
Spend more time with our children				
Work late				
Get together with his/her friends				
Discipline children				
Help with homework				
Give me attention when I need it				
Pay attention to my sexual needs				
Assume responsibility for finances				
Leave me time to myself				
Agree to do things I like				
Express his/her emotions clearly				
Accomplish responsibilities promptly				
Spend time with me				
Come to meals on time				
Want to go to church with me				

I Would Like My Partner To:	Satisfied	Less	More	Major Item
Be sensitive to my thoughts and feelings				
Be patient with me				
Over look my mistakes				
Take time in lovemaking				
Spend time at home				
Work on personal hygiene and cleanliness				
Be direct with me				
See the need to fix things				
Wear clothing to bed				

Items for Your Marriage Partner

I Would Like My Partner To:	Satisfied	Less	More	Major Item
Manage money wisely				
Spend time keeping the house clean				
Have meals ready on time				
Pay attention to grooming and appearance				
Get together with friends				
Prepare interesting meals				
Show appreciation for things I do				
Get together with my relatives				
Have sexual relations with me				
Spend more time with our children				
Work late				

I Would Like My Partner To:	Satisfied	Less	More	Major Item
Get together with his/her friends				
Discipline children				
Help with homework				
Give me attention when I need it				
Pay attention to my sexual needs				
Assume responsibility for finances				
Leave me time to myself				
Agree to do things I like				
Express his/her emotions clearly				
Accomplish responsibilities promptly				
Spend time with me				
Come to meals on time				
Want to go to church with me				
Be sensitive to my thoughts and feelings				
Be patient with me				
Over look my mistakes				
Take time in lovemaking				
Spend time at home				
Work on personal hygiene and cleanliness				
Be direct with me				
See the need to fix things				
Wear clothing to bed				

NOTES

1. Ellen Kreidman, *Light Her Fire* (New York: Dell Publishing, 1991), 11.
2. Laura Schlessinger, *The Proper Care and Feeding of Marriage* (Harper Collins, 2007), 11.

Communicating in Your Marriage and Family

A WOMAN IN one of my university marriage classes wrote the following description of the way she and her husband communicate with each other in their greetings and good-byes:

> We have a routine at the door before leaving each morning. It's not something we planned to do, but something that happened spontaneously, felt good, and so we automatically continue to do it. For about five minutes before we leave, we hug and kiss (etc!) at the door, complimenting each other in some ways (clothes, hair, jewelry, the night before, a recent achievement) and then we wish each other luck on a specific task to be done at work (a conference with "negative" parents for me, installing an antennae up a 100′ tree for him, etc.)
>
> When I get home first, I pick up the mail, turn on the porch and living room lights and freshen myself up. I set the table and begin dinner, hoping to get it in the oven before he comes. Our reunion in the evening is as exciting as our morning farewell! I try to get to the door empty-handed and open-armed.

Wow, what a romantic marriage.

Although every couple does not necessarily need this style of communication for an enjoyable relationship, all need to establish patterns of communication that work for them.

In describing what's wrong with their marriage, some people

say, "We just don't communicate." Clearly, a lack of good communication can cause a relationship to wither on the vine, so to speak, and such partners gradually become strangers to each other.

It is, however, literally impossible for two people to live together and not communicate in one way or another. Avoiding each other's company, remaining silent when together, or refusing to respond to a family member's efforts to communicate—stonewalling—all signal a message of disinterest, dislike, or even disdain. Communication proceeds continuously in every close relationship, and its major theme is either negative or positive.

SEND A CLEAR MESSAGE

No matter how you are communicating, whether face-to-face or by writing notes, emails, and text messages, the most important rule of good communication is to send a clear message. This can best be done by using the personal pronoun "I." When sending a message to your marriage partner or other family member, start by referring to yourself. Say "I like . . ." "I dislike . . ." "I would like . . ." "I like it when you . . ." "I wish you would . . ." "I wish you would not . . ." or "I want you to . . ."

In his book *Sexual and Marital Health*, Dr. Clark Vincent describes the communication of a husband and wife who have not learned the art of sending a clear message. Instead, their messages are loaded with fuzzy uncertainties:

John: Honey, would you like to go out for dinner? (Mary is wild to get out of the house and to enjoy a good dinner she hasn't had to prepare, but, seeing and hearing John's fatigue, she responds in low key.)

Mary: Well, if you would like to.

John: What do you think?

Mary: If you want to—yes. (After a varying number of what-do-you-want-to-do's, they find themselves in the car.)

John: Where would you like to eat? (Mary would love to eat at a decent restaurant for a change, but, thinking of John's fatigue and their finances, she remains noncommittal.)

Mary: Wherever you would like to eat.

John: I'll take you wherever you want to go. You are sure it makes no difference to you?

Mary: Well, wherever suits you. I'm just glad to be out of the house. (This lethargic exchange continues until they find themselves at the local "greasy spoon" restaurant. Throughout the dinner John is puzzled and eventually feels defeated by her obvious lack of enthusiasm and enjoyment)[1]

Don't expect your marriage partner and other family members to read your mind. Instead, send a clear message of what you want. Remember, you are far more likely to get what you want in your marriage if you say what you want.

Regularly making brief telephone calls, emails, or text messages to family members at home and even at work when acceptable can improve communication and feelings of closeness. This is especially important when daily schedules limit the amount of time between husbands and wives, parents and children. An easy, fast message can help close many communication gaps.

If a message is to be useful, it must not only be clearly sent, it must also be received, understood, and appreciated. Three factors that influence how well a message will be received are **timing, setting**, and **manner**.

Each of us listens better and comprehends more accurately when the time is right and the setting and manner of communicating are pleasant. No matter how careful we are to send a clear message, we may get busy signals instead of an open line of communication if we use bad timing. If I sense that a family member is concentrating on a project and has a limited time to complete it, I'm going to wait for a better time to communicate my message—provided it's the kind of message that can wait.

Timing: Good timing means that I don't interrupt when others are speaking. Good timing also means that I delay the attempt to communicate an important message if it is obvious that the listener would not be receptive for some other reasons, such as being hungry, tired, or upset.

Setting: An appropriate setting for controversy and for attempting to resolve an issue of controversy would be a room that is comfortable, pleasant, and private. An adequate communication setting might also be the office of a professional marriage and family therapist or your clergyman.

Manner: If you are to send a clear message, you need to learn to vary the volume of your voice, depending on the distance between you and your listener, and the amount of noise pollution that is present. You and I have the responsibility to use a sufficient volume of voice to be heard both in conversation and public speaking. Move as close to your listener as would be appropriate, depending on the nature of your relationship. Then you will not need to shout—unless there is a lot of noise pollution. Being close, you are able to not only moderate your volume of speech, but also use a more pleasant tone of voice.

Probably nothing is more effective in eliciting goodwill and in generating feelings of kindness than a pleasant tone of voice. On the other hand, a negative tone of voice will usually bring a negative response from your listener. Even though our message is true and is spoken with clever words, it will not be well received if we have an offensive tone of voice. Have you noticed on the telephone how some people have a smile in their voice and others a frown? Your marriage partner and other family members will assess your mood by your tone of voice and arrive at various conclusions such as, "You're glad to see me," "You feel indifferent about me," "You are pleased (or displeased) with me," or "You feel energetic (or tired, happy, or sad)."

Occasionally, video recording conversations with your marriage partner or other family members can motivate each of you to improve your manner of communicating. Knowing that you are being recorded will hopefully motivate you to make a special effort to choose your words and tone of voice carefully. This can help you improve your marriage and family life because what you say and how you say it have a profound influence on the quality of your relationships.

Are You Listening?

Along with sending a clear message, nothing is more important in communication than listening carefully and then responding to what you've heard. Be an honest listener. Do not feign attention. If someone begins to speak to you, and you either cannot or do not want to listen at that moment, say, "I want to hear what you have to say, but I can't listen now." This is being honest with yourself and with the person who wants to tell you something.

When you are ready to listen, focus your attention fully on what is being said and pay attention to the body language as well as to the spoken word. As listeners, you and I have a definite responsibility to give some kind of response to what we hear. Only when we respond or reply can the person doing the talking know that we have heard and understood the intended message.

We can enhance the quality of our responses by doing reflective listening or by "mirroring back." This involves intermittently summarizing in our minds what we think the message is and then briefly stating it back to the speaker. Our feedback lets him or her know whether we comprehend the message.

Overs and Unders

Two undesirable ways of responding to something someone says or does are overreacting and underreacting. When we respond immediately to a message by expressing strong disapproval or anger, we risk damaging the rapport in our relationship. On the other hand, we may leave the sender of a message with an empty, disappointed feeling when we underreact—responding with only a murmur or a ho-hum type of statement that expresses boredom.

Writing notes as you listen to your marriage partner or another family member gives an important message that you are trying to listen carefully, and remember what you have heard. The mild exercise of writing can help you remain alert.

Body Language

The body language that you and your family use to communicate will have a monumental influence on the quality of your relationships. When you are receiving as well as sending messages, move closer to your marriage partner or child, look at him or her, and be aware of your eyes, your facial expression, your tone of voice, and the power of touch. These six aspects of body language form the key word **CLEFTTO**:

C Getting **Closer**

L **Looking** at

E **Eyes**—as supermodel Heidi Klum would say, smile with your eyes. Positive thoughts about the person with whom you are relating will help you convey warm feelings

F **Facial Expression**

T **Tone of Voice**

T Appropriate **Touching**

O **Open Body Position**

Getting **close** attracts attention and gives a feeling of intimacy. However, if we are socially sensitive, we will position ourselves with varying degrees of distance from others, depending on the emotional closeness in the relationship. Caressing, patting, and hugging can be emotionally nourishing when used with discretion. Between friends, touch is a powerful way of saying, "I like you," and between loved ones it carries the message, "I love you."

Looking at the one to whom you're speaking prompts him or her to listen more intently and conveys a message of sincerity. Looking at someone who's telling you something is a way of saying, "I'm tuned in."

How we use our eyes can evoke a positive or negative response. The pupils of the eyes tend to dilate when we are communicating with someone we like. How does this affect the manner in which others respond to us? When people were shown a picture of a woman whose pupils were very constricted, she was judged to be cold and unfriendly, but after the same photograph was retouched to make this woman's eyes appear to be dilated, she was rated kind and friendly. Even when you're communicating with someone in your family about something negative, it will still be possible for you to think some positive thoughts about this person. Doing so will help your eyes have a pleasant appearance. This, in turn, will help the person with whom you are talking have a more positive feeling toward you.

Some **eye-to-eye contact** is important if we are to be taken seriously, but we can overdo it. Staring into someone's eyes might be interpreted as an invasion of privacy, and glaring could be felt as an attack. Whether you are speaking or listening, every few moments allow your gaze to drift elsewhere.

If we are not careful with our body language, the message it sends might preempt the words we speak. Richard Nixon lost his first debate with John F. Kennedy during the 1960 presidential campaign mainly because of his facial expression. A news commentator said he first heard the debate by way of radio and concluded that Nixon had won, but later, after seeing a replay of it on TV he said he could see why a majority of Americans who were polled believed that Kennedy had won. Nixon's forehead was furrowed and he looked worried, while Kennedy's face appeared pleasant and relaxed. A constant smile is not necessary, but a pleasant expression is important. Reminding oneself to relax will reduce tension and enhance one's expression.

TALK ABOUT TRIVIA IS OK

Many marriage partners get into a habit of saying very little to each other. Sometimes during the counseling process, one of the spouses says to the other, "You don't talk to me enough." In defense, the partner sometimes replies, "It's because I have nothing important to say." If you have a habit of saying very little to your wife or husband, you can break this habit and form a new, improved pattern of communicating. You can begin by talking even about trivia because it is easy to talk about. Comment on the weather, what you are watching on TV, or the book or magazine you are reading. Occasionally read a newspaper or magazine article aloud to give your partner an opportunity to respond to it. Every day tell your companion about at least one thing that happened at work or at home even though it might seem unimportant to you. The more you talk, the better you get to know each other's thoughts and feelings and the more you increase your level of intimacy. Caution: be sensitive to your partner's level of receptiveness and adjust your amount of talk accordingly. Be careful not to be a motor mouth. If you rattle on and on, your listener might become bored and tune you out.

Do You and Your Partner Talk Too Much?

The two of you are talking too much if you find yourselves repeatedly contending. To contend means to argue, dispute, and quarrel. If you are to keep contention to a minimum, you need to have a policy that you will not discuss certain things. One of the most harmful communication mistakes that lovers make is to think that they must discuss every topic. Your relationship will go more smoothly if you seldom discuss issues that are highly controversial between you, such as politics, religion, and your behavioral traits. Furthermore, I recommend that you seldom discuss a point of criticism or a complaint that the other partner has made. When these topics are discussed, the conversation often deteriorates into an argument.

Never miss an opportunity to shut up.

You can express your major ideas on a subject in less than five minutes, so keep it brief. Simply state your position and do not elaborate. Years ago I read somewhere the statement, "Lord, fill my mouth with good stuff, and nudge me when I've said enough." Remember, an understatement is more likely to be accepted than an overstatement.

Flooding contributes to stonewalling. Flooding is characterized by one partner or the other repeatedly criticizing and pestering. Flooding is nagging, and nagging is repeatedly urging, scolding, and fault-finding. The partner who feels flooded tends to retreat into silence and mentally put up a stone wall. In their research on love, John and Julie Gottman discovered that wives more often do flooding and husbands more often withdraw and stonewall. Husbands nag as well as wives, but not as often. When a man is nagging, women say he is controlling.

THREE C'S TO AVOID: CRITICIZING, COMPLAINING, AND CONTENDING

Some partners erroneously believe that if they can just communicate more, their relationship will become much better. Increasing the quantity of communication without being cautious about its quality can hurt feelings and create resentment. A proverb says everything we say should have to pass through three gates before we say it. At the first gate, the gatekeeper should ask, "Is it true?" At the second gate, "Is it necessary?" and at the third gate, "Is it kind?"

Criticizing, complaining, and contending are all communicated profusely in some families, simply as a matter of habit. In these homes, there is not so much a lack of communication as there is too much communication of the wrong kind.

Sometimes a couple can improve their relationship by tactful criticism and justifiable complaints. But I cannot think of a single instance in which contention has ever helped a relationship. Love relationships will be improved if partners will make a conscious effort to reduce the frequency of criticizing, complaining, and contending. Remember contending is arguing, disputing, and quarreling. I challenge you to endeavor to go three hours at a time without resorting to any of these three "C's." Try it. It's not easy. If you find three hours too difficult, then try two hours at a time or perhaps only one.

DISCUSSING CONFLICT ISSUES

Conflict in human relations is a strong disagreement. If one or both of you becomes angry, your talk should be temporarily terminated until emotional composure has been regained. If angry feelings intensify, get away from each other until your hostile feelings subside.

Communicating with your partner about your marriage has the potential for making your relationship better or worse. Communication that begins with a hope for better understanding and better feelings often deteriorates into just the opposite. A simple difference of opinion, a point of controversy, can be safely discussed in most marriages. But if your conversation has deteriorated to contention, to angry words and actions, then you are cautioned to consider three alternatives: Communicate in the company of a mediator, in writing, or by using the following talk guidelines. *Take turns* expressing your thoughts and feelings on the conflict issue. You can flip a coin to determine who gets to talk first. A *time limit* must be agreed upon, such as fifteen minutes for each person. Many homes and offices have clocks that chime every fifteen minutes. The one listening should speak only to ask occasional questions for clarification and to make brief statements to indicate understanding. Do mirroring or "reflective listening."

WRITING A MESSAGE IS SOMETIMES CLEARER AND SAFER THAN SPEAKING IT

If you want to communicate something to your marriage partner that you think might result in angry words or an argument, perhaps you should write your message instead of speaking it.

When you want to communicate to your partner that something about his or her behavior is bothering you, you can write four brief paragraphs as follows: (1) describe what's being done that annoys you, (2) explain how you feel about it, (3) specify the exact change that you would like, and (4) state what good consequences you believe will come from this improvement.[2]

A message that is written is more likely to be taken seriously than a quick statement, especially when a husband and wife are upset at each other about a certain issue. Keep in mind that your marriage partner and family members are more apt to accept your communications regarding negatives if you regularly communicate positives. Develop the habit of writing complimentary notes and occasionally write a love letter to your children as well as to your marriage partner.

Memos that are regularly exchanged in marriages and families can promote understanding and can produce a flow of information regarding adjustments that need to be made and tasks that need to be accomplished. There are several advantages to writing memos. They are a good way of complimenting, apologizing, and reminding because they can be read and reread by the recipient. Memos are a careful way of requesting changes in behavior. After writing a memo, you can read it, reconsider it, and perhaps rewrite it. You can also keep it for a few days and then either throw it away or give it to your partner when the timing and setting are right.

Partners can highlight or bracket parts of articles and books that they want each other to read. Some might find this technique especially useful for communicating their sexual likes and dislikes.

NOTES

1. Clark E. Vincent, *Sexual and Marital Health* (Nevato, California: McGraw Hill, 1973), 80–81.
2. Dr. John Gottman, et al. Couple's Guide to 1976.

9

Enriching Your Marriage
and Family

1+1=3

An enriched relationship, whether between a husband and wife, a parent and child, or friends and lovers is not a lucky accident. A happy vibrant relationship is an achievement. Whatever is good about a marriage is the creation of both the man and the woman; and whatever is not good is also their creation.

In marriage, one man plus one woman equals not two but three. The third element refers to the dynamics of their relationship, whether it is warm and friendly or cold and prickly, whether it is loving or unloving. Two logs in a fireplace might be smoldering or glowing. Many relationships are unnecessarily smoldering because of neglect.

In their book *We Can Have Better Marriages if We Really Want Them,* David Mace, cofounder of the Association for Couples in Marriage Enrichment, and his wife, Vera, say

> The enriched marriage did not get to be that way by accidental good fortune—it is always, as we understand it, the result of deliberate, enlightened effort on the part of both partners working together. The development of a really good marriage is not a natural process. It is an achievement.[1]

Dr. A. H. Chapman commented that

> It is a slow drifting into boredom which destroys a marriage so insidiously that neither marital partner knows what is happening. It is caused by perfunctory pecks on the cheek instead of passionate kisses, forgotten anniversaries and birthdays, hair that is always in curlers, sex that is wrestling instead of lovemaking, and a thousand forms of carelessness that never happened during the courtship but which began after the honeymoon.[2]

Rekindling Romantic Love

If a husband and wife are in serious conflict, their relationship may need a major "overhaul," but most couples just need a marriage "tune-up" from time to time.

Take time to do whatever it takes for a good marriage—time to talk, time to touch, and time to make love. Take time for romantic dates—take time for just the two of you together.

Most love partners want a romantic relationship. You can regularly rekindle your romantic feelings by having a special date together every other weekend, or at least once a month, and miniature honeymoon excursions three or four times a year. A three-day weekend together will usually be sufficient. Arrange a longer romantic getaway whenever possible.

Carol Amen tells of a couple who had the wisdom to renew the sparkle in their marriage by having a honeymoon-type weekend even though they could hardly afford it.

> When I was a student nurse, I baby-sat during off-duty hours to help pay my way. One day I got a call to sit for a whole weekend.
>
> All I knew when I headed for the job was that the couple wanted to get away from their two kids for a few days. Expecting that only rich people did that, I was surprised when their home turned out to be a tiny house in the borderline part of the city. Ted, the husband, had just joined an architectural firm. His wife, Ardeth, looked terribly tired. They waited . . . while I got acquainted with their children, 2 years and 11 months old. I held the baby against my shoulder while Ted gave me the name of their hotel. "You'll be there the whole time?" I asked.
>
> "That's headquarters," Ted answered. "We'll sleep late, prowl

around town, eat when we get hungry, visit the art galleries . . ." Mentally, I added up the cost of that, plus my fee. "But won't that be terribly expensive?" I blurted. I had adopted them already.

"Why, yes, I guess it will," Ted said. "But it's important. We're both tired and snapping at each other. Ardeth, especially, needs to get away from the children." Ardeth smiled at me. "Don't you know about hyacinths to feed the soul?" She took a volume from the bookcase and opened it to a poem called "Gulistan," by Muslin-uddin Sadi, a sheik who lived more than 700 years ago:

> If of thy mortal goods thou art bereft
> And from thy slender store two loaves alone to thee are left,
> Sell one, and with the dole
> buy hyacinths to feed the soul.

That poem taught me a great deal. Those two didn't have enough money for the trip, but they were tuned in on a set of values I'd never even thought of. Sunday night, when they came back, they looked like teen-agers who'd just discovered love. And my payment was tucked under the ribbon on a pot holding a lavender hyacinth.

Over the years since, I've made a hobby of noticing people and whether or not they know about using nonessentials and extravagances occasionally to feed the soul. The happiest people do.[3]

A good relationship is like a properly inflated tire. A neglected marriage is like a worn tire, low on air. Most marriages that go flat are not the result of a blowout but rather a slow leak. In such a marriage, usually both the husband and wife have neglected their relationship. Their marriage is like an untended fire. In fires, tires, and love relationships, little things can make a big difference.

21 WAYS TO ENHANCE THE ROMANCE IN YOUR MARRIAGE

- Relate to each other with courtesy, kindness, and respect.
- Take a moonlight walk.
- Play in the water together occasionally, in either the shower or the tub.
- Experience a weekend "honeymoon trip" from time to time.
- Identify mutual interests and activities that you both enjoy and participate in them together.

- Bring flowers home to your marriage partner and once in a while deliver them to his or her place of work.
- Write love notes and put them on the steering wheel of the car or somewhere else.
- Arrange a date and meet someplace new where you have never been before.
- Write and exchange a romantic "wish list."
- Go on a camping trip to the ocean.
- Shop together for romantically appealing clothing.
- Replace the bath soap you have always used with new scented bars.
- Walk together when it's raining or snowing.
- Read books together to rekindle your romantic and sexual love.
- Take dance lessons together.
- Write a love letter to your marriage partner at least once or twice a year.
- Pose together for romantic pictures at a photo studio.
- After a bedtime shower or bath, give each other a caress and massage treat before sleep.
- Rent a cabin in the woods or pitch a tent in the mountains where there is no radio, Internet, texting, TV, or newspaper.
- Frequently give compliments, express affection, and do something nice for your partner.
- Feelings that are repeatedly expressed become stronger. You will strengthen your feelings of love by often saying, "I love you." Plan to say, "I love you" at the beginning and end of each day, and sometimes say it in writing.

LOVE RITUALS IN YOUR MARRIAGE

In his book, *Take Back Your Marriage*, Dr. William Doherty talks about the value of love rituals. A ritual in marriage is an activity that a husband and wife do often together. Professor Doherty explains how he and his wife have a love ritual of visiting together in their hot tub; he tells of another couple whose ritual is to shower together just before bedtime.[4]

Various rituals can help a husband and wife regularly reconnect with each other and reinforce the bond between them.

I have a friendship with a couple in their eighties who walk together nearly every evening. A husband and wife can reromanticize their marriage by making a decision to emphasize the importance of their wedding anniversary. Our wedding anniversary is August 22. My wife and I can choose to make the 22 of each and every month a special day for us.

Think about the many Fourth of July rituals, including the "Star Spangled Banner" and John Philip Sousa march tunes, and how these rituals magnify our feelings of patriotism.

The following email was written to Dr. Laura in regard to a telephone call from a wife whose husband had neglected to remember their thirtieth wedding anniversary.

> The other day my wife and I had the good fortune to catch part of your show while driving home from work early. We heard the caller who was complaining about how her husband had completely ignored her 30th wedding anniversary. I find that hard to believe and thought you may appreciate a man's point of view.
>
> How could her husband possibly ignore the fresh cut flowers in the living room when he got home from work? How could he ignore the perfume she was wearing or the outfit she had on? Or that she had cooked his favorite meal, or in the least made reservations at their favorite restaurant. How could her husband possibly ignore the candles or the bath that she had drawn for them to share, or the lovemaking that followed such a wonderful evening? Or even the hotel reservations that she had booked for them.
>
> Oh . . . I know. . . . none of these things happened. She simply sat there and expected their anniversary to be another birthday party for her. She forgot that an anniversary is about celebrating their lives together, not an opportunity to get another piece of jewelry she had her eyes on. It isn't about things. It's about each other.
>
> I guess her husband didn't have much to celebrate.[5]

EAT TOGETHER MORE OFTEN

A typical day for most family members includes a wide divergence of destinations and time schedules. This active lifestyle makes it difficult for all the members of a family to eat meals together regularly. This is unfortunate because communication can be increased and even improved through mealtime conversation. Families would do well to establish daily routines in their homes that facilitate eating meals together. We use a dinner bell as a signal to our family members that a meal is ready. Without a bell in our three-level house, it would take a lot of shouting to inform our five children to "come and get it." Our family members respond better to a ringing bell than to a shout. In the evening at our home, especially at the dinner table, I sometimes like to invite family members to respond to the statement, "The highlight of my day was . . ." Our youngest daughter, Jennifer, has enjoyed this experience immensely; starting when she was four, she has regularly requested "highlights" at the table.

During these highlights, each family member is free to comment on at least one event of the day, but no one is required to do so. One's peak experience of the day is usually something simple like accomplishing a task, enjoying a meal, or receiving good news. This focus on highlights encourages family members to accentuate the positive aspects of their day's activities in their conversation. Of course, all family members know that they are also free to communicate about the "lowlights" of their day. Mealtime, however, is not a good time to talk habitually about negatives.

CONCLUSION

In marriages, families, and friendships, a happy, enriched relationship is never a lucky gift. It is an achievement that must be created and re-created through careful cooperative effort.

MARRIAGE ENRICHMENT MESSAGES, INVENTORY A

Most couples will discover that a good marriage can be even better if they will regularly speak and write messages to each other using the guidelines on the next three pages. You can communicate these important messages to your partner either by writing a letter or just by talking, and you can give your relationship a tune-up from time to time by rewriting and respeaking these messages. You will probably discover that your communication on most of these items will go more smoothly if you and your partner do not discuss the information that you exchange.

1. My impression of you when we first met was _____

_____

2. Highlights in our relationship that I like to remember are

_____

3. I'm glad that _____
4. I like your _____
5. I appreciate you for _____
6. I admire your _____
7. I like it when you _____
8. I think you show your love to me by _____
9. I think I show my love to you by _____
10. The ways that I think we are similar are

_____

11. The ways that I think we are different are

_____

12. The things in which I think you have greater ability than I have are _____
13. Good things I've learned from you are _____

_____

14. Things I like about you as a mother/father are

_____

15. Things I like about your parents, family members, and friends are _____
16. I would appreciate it if _____
17. I hope that I _____
18. I hope that we _____
19. I wish that you would _____
20. I would like you to _____

MARRIAGE ENRICHMENT MESSAGES, INVENTORY B

1. Discuss with your partner some of the things that you did today and this week that helped you think well of yourself.

2. Explain to your partner some of the things that you did today and this week to have a better relationship with him or her.

3. I felt especially close to you today or this week when

_____

4. Some of your virtues and qualities as a marriage partner are

_____

5. As my marriage partner, some of the most important things that I expect from you are _____

_____

6. In our relationship I need _____

7. In our marriage I would like _____

8. Concerning physical affection, I like _____

   I would like _____

9. Sexually, I like _____

   I would like _____

   I wish that _____

   I want _____

10. A problem in our relationship or in our family that I would like us to work on is _____

11. Something that I would like to ask you to forgive me for is

_____

12. Something I think you have never fully understood about me and my life is _____

13. Some of the goals that I have in mind for myself, for you, and for us are _____

_____

14. A plan of action that I think would help in the achievement of these goals is _____

_____

15. Tell your mate about certain married couples whose relationship you admire and explain why you admire their relationship. You will probably refer mainly to certain couples with whom you are mutually acquainted, but you can also refer to historical or contemporary famous couples.

16. One of the major strengths in our marriage is

_____

17. Reread together some of your love letters and look at your marriage and family photographs together.

18. Write your fantasy of a romantic holiday that you would like to take with your marriage partner.

PARENT-CHILD ENRICHMENT MESSAGES

Using the following lead-in statements along with any others that you can think of, write a letter to your son or daughter, or to your mom or dad. The purpose of doing this is to improve goodwill and warm feelings between you.

1. One of the things I like most about you is

_____

2. I appreciate your _____

3. I admire your _____

4. I like your _____

5. I like it when you _____

6. I think you show your love to me by _____

7. The ways that I think we are similar are

_____

8. The ways that I think we are different are

_____

9. The things in which I think you have greater ability than I have are _____

10. Good things that I've learned from you are

_____

11. I'm glad that _____

12. I hope that you _____

13. I wish that you would _____

14. I would like you to _____

15. I would appreciate it if _____

16. I want you to _____

17. Highlights in our relationship that I like to remember are

_____

NOTES

1. David and Vera Mace, *We Can Have Better Marriages if We Really Want Them* (Nashville, TN: Abingdon Press, 1975), quoted in A.H. Chapman, *Put-Offs and Come-Ons* (New York: Berkley Publishing, 1977).

2. Chapman, *Put-Offs and Come-Ons.*

3. Carol Amen, *Hyacinths to Feed the Soul*, (Nashville, TN: Southern Publishing Association, 1975).

4. William Doherty, PhD, *Take Back Your Marriage* (New York: The Guilford Press, 2003).

5. Laura Schlessinger, PhD, *The Proper Care and Feeding of Marriage*, (New York: Harper, 2007), 42–43.

10

Protecting and Strengthening

Your Marriage

BE A LOYAL ALLY

Most of us who are citizens of the USA are willing to say, "I pledge allegiance to the flag of the United States of America." A pledge is a promise, and to have allegiance to something or someone is to be true and loyal. Love partners, family members, and close friends can enrich and protect their relationships by thinking of themselves as allies. You can choose to have an attitude of having pledged yourselves to each other.

The word *ally* is Old French. It means a bond of friendship between a husband and wife or any two people, groups, or nations. We are more likely to have relationships that are warm and friendly if we know how to be a true ally. Here are some essentials of being a loyal ally:

- **ACCEPT**—Accept your marriage partner, or whomever, just as he or she is in every way. This important person in your life can—and probably will—make improvements; but for now, it is essential that this individual experience full acceptance.

- **ACCENTUATE THE POSITIVES**—Accentuate the positives about your loved one or friend. Most of us have experienced the benefits that can come into our lives by accentuating the positives instead of the negatives. Think of this person's qualities and strengths and frequently acknowledge them to him or her, especially in the company of others.

- **APPRECIATE**—You can warm the feelings of others and give them an emotional lift by often making statements to them such as, "I appreciate you for . . . ," "I admire you for your . . . ," and "I respect you for . . ."

- **ADMIRE**—We admire people who have worked hard to develop their talents and those who are successful in spite of difficult circumstances. Acknowledge the achievements of others to them.

- **AGREE**—As a true ally, it is important that you always listen for what you can agree with and for the underlying positive in what is being said. It is also important that you look for the underlying positive in what one is doing or is planning to do. Your husband or wife will want to be with you only if you help this person feel good about himself or herself.

- **AFFIRM AND VALIDATE**—People will think of you as their ally and will want to be your ally if you affirm and validate them. Because you have an affirmative attitude, you take time to give a hearty greeting or to walk across a room or a street to give a friendly hand clasp with an inquiry about a person's well-being. Telephone calls, greeting cards, letters, and "being there" are all actions of affirmation.

Whenever your husband or wife is complimenting, correcting, or teaching one or more of your children and you agree with what is being said, you can affirm and validate your partner by immediately speaking words of agreement. You will magnify your parent power and your children's respect for both of you if you endorse and support your partner in the presence of your children. Likewise you will enrich and protect your other family relationships and your friendships by affirming and validating these people, especially when in the company of others.

As an ardent ally and loyal friend, we endeavor to be there when someone important to us is dancing, singing, speaking, competing as an athlete, or performing in any other way. Being there is imperative in times of illness, injury, or loss.

In explaining the qualities of an authentic ally, I have chosen words that start with the letter "A." There is another "A" word that needs to be included: apologies. Many years ago, I heard a military officer say to his ROTC students, "Never apologize. It is a sign of weakness." He was wrong. A sincere apology is a sign of strength. Never underestimate the power of an apology in human relations.

Consider this woman's description of her parent's loyalty to each other.

> The trait I admired most growing up was my mother's unwavering loyalty to my father. To the world, they presented a consolidated whole: respectful of each other, always each other's first priority. As a child, I wanted to be the center of my parents' universe. But my parents were, and are, each other's universe and we children remain merely sources of light that shine upon their special world. Only as an adult can I appreciate the fact that, although loved, we were not chosen in the way my parents chose each other.

Marriages that were deteriorating toward divorce have been saved because the partners reversed their relationship-defeating attitudes and actions and decided to become each other's loyal ally.

An example is a religious couple with three young children. They were on the verge of divorce when the wife contacted our marriage counseling office for an appointment. She came in to determine what could be done to dissuade her husband from divorce. He then came in to explain why he was divorcing her and why he had moved out of their home eight months earlier.

This husband spoke with firm conviction that he had decided to divorce his wife even though he felt sad about it and was concerned about their children. It was clear that he was experiencing her as one who was not his ally but just the opposite.

This woman accepted my challenge to more fully become her husband's loyal ally—to experiment with new ways of relating to her husband and to accept him in every way just as he is. She was taught to magnify his qualities and minimize his deficiencies in her thoughts and to express appreciation to him every day, occasionally letting him know that she admires him. She was also taught when he is talking to her to listen for what she can agree with instead of listening for what she can disagree with. She was further taught to look for what she could approve of in what he was doing or planning to do. This wife deserves to be commended for her success in applying the principles of being a true ally.

Every man wants his wife to be his ally and every woman wants her husband to be her ally. Decide now that you will always be an ally, a true friend, a fan, and a cheerleader for everyone in your life that is precious to you.

Her new style of relating to her husband brought her the miracle that she wanted in her marriage. Within a few days of more fully being his ally, he hugged and kissed her for the first time in eight months. He also decided to return home to his wife instead of divorcing her.

The marriage is the heart of the family; therefore, in most homes, as the marriage goes, so goes the family. The surest way to create a good happy family is to create and re-create a good, happy marriage.

Your marriage is the heart of your family; therefore, the best thing a man can do for his children is to love his wife, and the best thing a woman can do for her children is to love her husband.

We can compare relationships in a family to a wagon wheel. You can think of your marriage as the hub of the wheel and each child or any other family member who resides in your home as a spoke on your family wagon wheel.

Many husbands and wives are neglecting their own relationship while they focus their time and attention on their children, friends, and various activities. Remember your marriage is the heart of your family. It is the hub of your home.

The 5:1 Ratio

In their Seattle Love Lab, Dr. John Gottman and his wife, Dr. Julie Gottman, have observed the relationships of many hundreds of married couples. They have concluded that couples that maintain happiness in their marriages are those who communicate five times more positives than negatives; this includes body language as well as the spoken word.

> Happily married couples behave like good friends. Their relationships are characterized by respect, affection and empathy and they pay close attention to what's happening in each other's lives. Studies of couples discussing conflict topics demonstrate this well. Spouses in happy, stable marriages made five positive remarks for every one negative remark when they were discussing conflict. In contrast, couples headed for divorce offered less than one positive remark for every single negative remark. Happily married couples handled conflict in gentle, positive ways. They recognized that some conflict is inevitable, but they don't get gridlocked in separate positions. Instead they keep talking to each other. They listen respectfully to each other, and find compromises that work for both of them.[1]

DEVELOPING EMPATHIC LOVE

Your loved ones and friends are more likely to esteem you as a true ally if you relate to them with empathy. Empathy is a special way of listening and responding to what we are hearing. It is tuning into an individual's thoughts and feelings. Empathic friends and lovers give focused attention, make eye contact, and relate back to the speaker a brief summary of what is being heard. This is referred to as reflective listening, or mirroring. It is as though we are holding up a mirror and reflecting back another person's message to us.

Acknowledging and accepting someone's opinions does not necessarily mean that we fully agree with these ideas. However, people are more likely to enjoy our company if we make a decision to have a policy of listening for what we can agree with instead of listening for what we can disagree with. We would do well to listen for the underlying positive in what someone is saying. We also need to look for the positive in what a person is doing or would like us to do instead of reaching a negative conclusion. For example, if another person wants you to use safety belts or to eat nutritious food and exercise regularly, you will protect the quality of your relationship by responding with a positive, appreciative attitude instead of with a negative, resentful attitude.

When we are sensitive to an individual's feelings and thoughts and that person knows that we know how he or she feels because of our manner of responding to him or her, we are being empathic and compassionate. Compassion is akin to empathy. A passion is a feeling. Being compassionate is being emotionally sensitive and supportive. Everyone who has developed the art of empathic love and friendship is compassionate and sympathetic whenever appropriate.

"PLEASANT WORDS ARE AS A HONEYCOMB"

The quality of a food can be enriched and improved by adding certain vitamins and minerals to it. The quality of human relations can also be enriched and improved by the thoughts we think, the words we speak, and the actions we take.

To protect and enhance our relationships, most of us need to be much more careful with what we say and how we say it. Words can heighten love or hurt it. Words can enhance friendship or encumber it. Words can build love or burden it. With our words, we can caress or crush. The terms *purring, snarling, warm fuzzies,* and *cold pricklies* are most often used in reference to the spoken word, but they can pertain to body language as well. Complimenting, encouraging, apologizing, smiling, winking, caressing, patting, hugging, and making statements such as, "I'm glad you came with me," "I want to thank you for . . . ," and "I love you" are all warm fuzzies, or purring-type expressions. Criticizing, putting down, labeling, frowning, stomping one's feet, and slamming doors are all cold pricklies, or snarling types of communication. Enriched, enjoyable relationships are comprised of people who do more complimenting than criticizing and complaining, and who do more smiling than frowning.

Proverbs in the Old Testament tells us, "Pleasant words are as an honeycomb, sweet to the soul, and health to the bones,"[2] and, "A word fitly spoken is like apples of gold in pictures of silver."[3]

"If you have something nice to say, say it with flowers." This is from a radio commercial of a greenhouse and floral shop. A gift

81

of flowers is a good way to express positive feelings. However, if we have something nice to say, it is even more important that we express it with words, both written and spoken. There is a song that says, "The kind words we give shall in memory live. . . . Let us oft speak kind words to each other; kind words are sweet tones of the heart."[4]

QUALITIES AND QUIRKS

There is no marriage so good that it cannot be better. There are few marriages so bad that they are hopeless. Think how creative you were when you were dating and courting. Remember how careful you were to arrange fun activities and to be ready on time. Remember how you did something special on Valentine's Day and for other important occasions. Making half as much effort now could revitalize your marriage. Cooperative, creative loving by a husband and wife will transform most marriages.

Actions that can undermine the vitality and romance of marriages include

- giving perfunctory pecks on the cheek instead of passionate kisses
- watching television instead of talking or making love
- having affectionate feelings without expressing them
- thinking thoughts of admiration and appreciation without saying them
- forgetting anniversaries and birthdays
- speaking with rudeness and anger
- remaining resentful
- being indifferent
- acting as though you don't care
- workaholism

These mistakes are seldom made during courtship. However, for many couples, they begin soon after the honeymoon. They are catalysts of erosion that can steadily undermine the foundation of a stable, happy marriage.

Attitudes and Behaviors That Can Undermine the Happiness of Your Marriage

Dr. John Gottman describes undesirable behavior between a husband and wife that propels the marriage into a downward spiral. If these marriage-defeating behaviors continue, many marriages eventually plummet into a divorce court.

Contempt is the most damaging attitude that contributes to a marriage going into a downward spiral and deteriorating toward divorce. Contempt is an attitude of disapproval, disdain, and disgust against each other. Contempt has the potential for double damage when both the husband and the wife have an attitude of contempt against the other.

Flooding: When Dr. Gottman speaks of flooding, he is referring to extreme and volatile anger that is sometimes characterized by name-calling, swearing, threatening, and foul language. A behavior of some partners who do intense flooding is to act as a verbal sniper. There are two versions of flooding: mild and severe. I think nagging is a form of mild flooding.

Stonewalling: The partner who feels flooded tends to retreat into silence and mentally put up a stone wall. In their research on marriage, John and Julie Gottman discovered that wives more often do flooding and husbands more often withdraw and stonewall.

Criticism is usually more destructive than a mere complaint. A complaint is usually focused on some negative circumstance in the lives such as a car they cannot rely on. In contrast, criticism tends to focus on behavioral patterns and personality traits. This is why criticism has the potential for more damage to the marriage than a complaint.

Defensiveness: The more we are criticized, the more we are inclined to be defensive. A better response for growth would be to learn how we can improve based on the criticism we receive.[5]

ABC WINESS

1. **Anger:** Anger that is fast, strong, and long.
2. **Blaming:** Habitually blaming your partner for things that

go wrong, even though he or she might have had nothing to do with it. Each of us needs to make a decision to do a "blame-ectomy."

3. **Criticizing, Complaining, and Contending:** These three "C's" can undermine and erode the happiness of a marriage. Complementing, praising, and building up one another are better than criticizing and putting down. Speaking cheerfully instead of complaining and trying to agree instead of arguing impulsively are also better.

4. **Withdrawal:** Withdrawal is done in various ways, such as walking away when your partner wants to talk, avoiding being where you know he or she is going to be, and going to bed unreasonably early or staying up until you are quite sure your marriage partner is asleep.

5. **Invalidating:** Minimizing and discounting the importance of what your partner is saying or doing. Dr. Howard Markman, coauthor of *Fighting for Your Marriage*, explains, "Invalidation hurts. It leads naturally to covering up who you are and what you think, because it becomes just too risky to do otherwise. People naturally cover up their innermost feelings when they believe that they will be 'put down.' Our research shows that invalidation is one of the very best predictors of future problems and divorce. Interestingly, the amount of validation in a relationship doesn't say as much about its health as the amount of invalidation does. Invalidation is a highly toxic poison to the well-being of your relationship."[6]

6. **Negative Interpretations:** The bad habit of giving a negative interpretation of what your husband or wife has said or done even though most people would see it as a good thing. For example, if a husband is being affectionate, we hope his wife will respond with appreciation instead of suspicion that he is trying to warm her up for sex.

7. **Escalating.** Intensifying arguments by thinking of what you can disagree with instead of thinking of what you can *agree* with, and intensifying anger by expressing anger strongly

with words and actions.[7]

8. **Separate Calendars**—Participating in fun activities and significantly important events without inviting your marriage partner or loved one to join with you. Wouldn't you agree that your marriage partner should be the most important person in the world to you? Your partner will know that you believe this only if you include him or her in most of your important events and recreational activities. Most enjoyment, fun, and laughter should include your marriage partner or fiancé.

9. **Neglecting Sexual Love**—Often not taking time for sexual love or ignoring your partner's erotic desires.

There is an increase in the incidence of adultery on the part of young wives as well as young husbands. Adultery can be devastating to the happiness and stability of a marriage.

The three R's of adultery are:

1. Resenting your marriage partner for one or more reasons.
2. Rendezvousing with someone who is attractive and appealing to you.
3. Rationalizing that you are justified in rendezvousing secretively with this person of the other sex whom you find to be a good listener and to have a fascinating personality.

PRINCIPLES FOR MAKING MARRIAGE WORK

Dr. John Gottman and his group of researchers have done extensive research to predict whether a couple will divorce. He says, "The most rewarding findings to come out of my studies are the 'Seven principles that will prevent a marriage from breaking up.'"

The following is a list of his principles with a brief explanation from the book, *The Seven Principles for Making Marriage Work.*[8]

1. **Enhance Your Love Maps.** "Emotionally intelligent couples are intimately familiar with each other's world. I call this having a richly detailed love map. . . . Another way of saying this is that these couple have made plenty of cognitive room

for their marriage. They remember the major events in each other's history and they keep updating this information as the facts and feelings of their spouse's world change."

2. **Nurture Your Fondness and Admiration.** "By simply reminding yourself of your spouse's positive qualities—even as you grapple with each other's flaws—you can prevent a happy marriage from deteriorating. The simple reason is that fondness and admiration are antidotes for contempt."

   I would add, live your life so that it is easy for your partner to admire you and respect you. Relate to him or her in ways that engender feelings of fondness for you.

3. **Turn Toward rather than Away.** "In marriage people periodically make what I call 'bids' for their partner's attention, affection, humor or support. People either turn toward one another after these bids or they turn away. Turning toward is the basis of emotional connection, romance, passion and a good sex life."

4. **Let Your Partner Influence You.** This has to do with Gottman's explanation of the importance of sharing power in the relationship. He has extensively explained the need for sharing in decision making. He especially emphasizes the importance of a husband accepting influence from his wife.

5. **Solve Your Solvable Problems.** Dr. Gottman has come up with a model for resolving conflict as a result of his research. His recommendations entail the following steps: "(1) Make sure your startup is soft rather than harsh, (2) learn the effective use of repair attempts, (3) monitor your physiology during tense discussions for warning signs of flooding, (4) learn how to compromise and (5) become more tolerant of each other's imperfections."

6. **Overcome Gridlock Problems** where you are "entrenched in your positions and unwilling to budge. . . . The goal in ending gridlock is not to solve the problem, but to move from gridlock to dialogue. The gridlocked conflict will probably always be a perpetual issue in your marriage, but one day you will be able to talk about it without hurting

each other. You will learn to live with the problem." You agree to disagree.

7. **Create Shared Meaning.** "A crucial goal of any marriage . . . is to create an atmosphere that encourages each person to talk honestly about his or her convictions. The more you speak candidly and respectfully with each other, the more likely there is to be a blending of your sense of meaning."[9]

NOTES

1. Gottman, *The Seven Principles of Making Marriage Work* (New York: Crown Publisher, 1999).
2. Proverbs 16:24, King James Version
3. Proverbs 25:11, King James Version.
4. *Hymns*. "Let Us Oft Speak Kind Words."
5. These are terms used in the research and writing of J. Gottman, PhD, et al. in *The Seven Principles of Making Marriage Work*.
6. Howard Markman, Scott Stanley, and Susan Blumberg, *Fighting for Your Marriage: Positive Steps for Preventing Divorce and Preserving a Lasting Love* (San Francisco: Jossey-Bass, 2001), 19.
7. Withdrawing, invalidating, negative interpretations, and escalating are terms resulting from the research and writing of Markman, et al., *Fighting For Your Marriage*.
8. Gottman and Silver, *The Seven Principles for Making Marriage Work*.
9. Ibid.

11

Sexual Love in Your Marriage

G OOD MARRIAGES CAN be enhanced and weak marriages strengthened by an improvement in the realm of physical love.

Dr. Eric Berne said, "Sex is an aid to happiness and work, a substitute for all manner of drugs and a healer of many sorts of sickness. It is for fun, pleasure and ecstasy. It binds people together with cords of romance, gratitude and love and it produces children." Even though sex has all this potential for good, a considerable number of happily married couples are sexually dissatisfied, and for couples whose marriages are on the rocks, many of the rocks are in their bed.

"Sex is an extremely important part of marriage. When it's good it offers couples opportunities to give and receive physical pleasure, to connect emotionally and spiritually. It builds closeness, intimacy and a sense of partnership. It defines their relationship as different from all others. Sex is a powerful tie that binds."[1]

DIVINELY CREATED

Men and women have been endowed by the eternal Creator with an ability to have continual sexual interest. Feelings of love can be renewed and revitalized by the sharing of erotic pleasure. The sexual experience between a husband and wife can strengthen their marriage bond. The sexual orgasm is associated with physiological changes throughout the body that increase positive feelings and decrease negative feelings. Thus God, in His wisdom, has given husbands and wives sex, for strengthening feelings of love as well as for reproduction.

Scriptural support for sexual enjoyment is found in the Old Testament, "Rejoice with the wife of thy youth . . . and be thou ravished always with her love."[2]

The Creator has given women as well as men an anatomical and physiological makeup so they are capable of having an ongoing sexual interest and desire. The sexual experience has the potential to create and re-create profound feelings of love and affection between a husband and wife. It also has the ability to reduce feelings of annoyance, irritability, and anger.[3] Furthermore, loving sex releases endorphins which create euphoria, an emotional high. It also releases oxytocin, a bonding and attachment hormone. We want strong emotional bonds between a husband and wife.

Candlelight and Silverware—What You See and Hear, and How You Look

Sex is not an entirely physical experience any more than eating a formal dinner is. The linen, candlelight, silverware, music, and conversation lend a cultural, social, and psychological embellishment to a dinner. Likewise, a good sexual relationship should also give one a feeling of well-being and euphoria. One's mind-set prior to and after an experience of lovemaking is important. Physical features such as cleanliness, good grooming, and attractive dress cannot be separated from what happens to one emotionally, psychologically, and spiritually pertaining to sexual relations. If one is to have vitality in his marriage, he must make an effort to be appealing to his partner. Uncouth table manners, halitosis, and one hundred and one more negligent acts contribute to each person's being disenchanted with the other and to the atrophy of the sexual relationship.

Dr. Charlie W. Shedd, a distinguished marriage and family relations author, tells of visiting with a wife in her home. "One afternoon at five, I was calling on a church member when she suddenly stood up, turned toward the door and said, 'Now, if you will excuse me, Dr. Shedd, John comes home in half an hour and I always spend the last thirty minutes before he arrives getting myself ready for him.'"[4]

A husband and wife can do certain things to get ready for their evening reunion. Most of us touch up a bit before seeing anyone whom we consider to be important, and no one is more important in your life than your marriage partner.

A husband may get up on Saturday morning and say to himself, "Well, let's see—I'm not going to work today, so I'll just put on this old pair of pants and this dirty shirt with the torn sleeves, and I won't bother to shave this morning. In fact, I won't have to shave all weekend." A wife who has been married for years may have hardly ever put on an attractive dress since taking off her wedding gown. She may go around in jeans most of the time and have her hair done up in curlers and then wonder why her husband lacks erotic interest in her. A husband wrote the following complaint:

> Dear Abby:
> I know you can't publish every letter you receive, but even though this is a very delicate subject, I hope you will print it, as it contains a very important message for many wives. Perhaps I should be completely honest and confess that it is meant for my own wife whom I cannot bring myself to tell.
> Wives write to you by the dozens, complaining that they do not get the physical love they need. Have they ever considered that perhaps there is a reason? I know of no better way to say this than "feminine hygiene." Nothing turns a man on quicker than a freshly bathed, sweet-smelling woman. And nothing turns him off quicker than one who is not.
> I love my wife, she keeps a spotless house, and a man couldn't want a better mother for his children. But she is careless about her person. I realize that she is tired, but if she would add 10 minutes to her day by taking a bath, dabbing on a little body powder, and a dab of cologne, she could add years to our love life. Believe me I know.
> "Turned Off" in Texas

For every man who would echo this complaint about his wife, there is a woman who would make a similar complaint about her husband. One wife wrote,

Dear Abby:

Why doesn't someone write something telling husbands that maybe they should be careful about how they look and smell or they might lose their wives?

A wife is supposed to be freshly bathed, immaculately groomed, fragrantly scented, with hair shining, and her breath as fresh as morning dew when her man comes home from work. Then he sits down to eat supper in his dirty work clothes after which he plops down in an easy chair and watches television until they play the Star Spangled Banner. Then he falls into bed without bathing or brushing his teeth and expects instant romance. I'd like to hear from other women to whom this scene is familiar.

GETTING READY

Getting ready for sex begins at the breakfast table and continues throughout the day in the overall way in which a husband and wife relate to one another.

The most important sex organ of the body is the brain. Getting oneself and one's partner ready for sex is as much psychological as it is physical. That's why sex begins at the breakfast table. How a husband and wife greet each other in the morning and treat each other the rest of the day will prepare their minds for sex or against it.

Sex therapy specialists teach that there is no such thing as an uninvolved spouse. Each partner contributes to the sexual response and enjoyment of the other. However, each person must take the main responsibility for charging his or her own sexual batteries and for learning to enjoy sexual orgasm.

A LANGUAGE OF LOVE

Sex in itself is a language of love, and its quality is influenced by the language one speaks to his marriage partner. Barnyard- or alley-type words spoken by one partner in reference to the genitals and sexual experience might be offensive and cheapen the experience for the other partner. In contrast, words of love and appreciation spoken to a marriage partner during lovemaking are vitalizing to the aura of romance. Using terms like frigid, impotent, and under-sexed will not help a partner improve sexual response.

Sexual pleasure and enjoyment are not only experienced in a

man's or woman's genitals—they are also manifested in one's mind, ego, self-esteem, and spirit.

THE POWER OF A KISS

For sexual renewal, a husband and wife must have a desire to create a sexual desire. One of the best ways to create a sexual desire in marriage is to often look lovingly into each other's eyes and kiss passionately. For most people, sensual kissing is sexually arousing. The word *kiss* comes from a Hebrew word which means to kindle a flame. Keep kissing.

SEXUAL SENSITIVITY

In marriage, we need to develop what may be referred to as sexual sensitivity. For example, if a wife says to her husband, "I feel too restless to sleep," it may be her way of saying to him, "I would like an erotic tonic." An insensitive husband might reply, "Well, since you can't sleep, why don't you get up and watch television?" If one partner says to the other, "I guess you are pretty tired tonight," what he or she may be saying is, "I hope you are not too tired for sex."

Every one of us needs to be tuned in to the undertones and subtle meanings of a marriage partner's comments and reply and respond in favor of more frequent erotic tonics in marriage.

SCHEDULING AND RATIONING

Most couples develop some kind of sexual schedule in their marriage, but it should not be followed rigidly. One who says to the partner, "Leave me alone, it's only been three days," is too schedule-minded. A smart man or woman does not ration his or her partner as to frequency. A spouse who thinks that all sexual love should be restricted to weekends, nighttime, and the bedroom with no variation, needs to develop a more playful attitude. But, if children or other family members are at home, surely a couple would have the discretion to make love in their bedroom with the door locked.

BARGAINING

Love and sex should not be placed on the bargain counter. I

counseled with a young couple who were bargaining with each other. The wife said, "I've hired lawyer and am suing Jack for divorce because he seldom expresses affection and he won't help around the house." I asked Jack why he didn't express love to his wife or assist with the household chores. He said, "Because Linda is sexually resistant. She won't let me touch her." When I asked Linda why she did not respond to her husband's sexual advances, she replied, "Because he does not express love to me and does not help around the house." Each one was waiting for the other. The wife had placed sex on the bargain counter and was in essence saying to her husband, "When you give me love, I will give you sex." The husband had placed love on the bargain counter saying, "When you give me sex, I will then give you love." Both love and sex should be freely given with no strings attached. When we bargain with love, holy wedlock becomes unholy deadlock.

THE "PETTER" AND THE "PETTEE"

In sexually troubled marriages, sex therapists have found in many cases that the husband or wife has the attitude that in love-making the husband should be the active "petter" and the wife should be the passive "pettee." This mistaken idea seems to be that sex is something that a husband does to his wife. Sex is not something that one person does to another. It is a physical, mental, and emotional sharing. Both must be active participants if it is to be mutually satisfying.

Some people might still have the old-fashioned, erroneous attitude that the husband is to do the seeking and the wife is to be sought after, that he pursues and she is pursued, or that he persists and she resists. A woman who is making an effort to have a high level of happiness in her marriage will not always wait for her husband to make the first move. She will often initiate sexual love with her husband and talk him into it. In playing the game of hide-and-seek, no person would enjoy having to do the seeking all of the time. It's got to be a boost to your ego to know that your partner has a strong enough sexual desire for you that he or she regularly pursues you for sexual love.

PERSUASION

Feeling a need for an "erotic tonic," one mate decides, "Tonight is the night," but the husband or wife might have other plans. Ideally one will respond promptly to a partner's sexual requests, but people do not perform ideally, so either the husband or the wife may need to persuade the other. One subtly communicates a desire, and if the partner does not respond with immediate enthusiasm, he or she sometimes withdraws into a state of cantankerous self-pity. Persistence and persuasion will bring a much more cooperative response from the partner than resentment and self-pity.

In conclusion, when requesting changes in sexual behavior, it is important that you begin your statements with phrases such as, "I would like" and "I wish that you would." Do not ask your partner to promise you to always do something or to never again do something else. Wanting to please you, your spouse might make a promise but later falter in keeping it. Broken promises reduce self-respect and goodwill. It is safer for you to make your expectations clear and then hope they will be complied with. For the same reason, adults need to avoid asking youth to promise to never again do something such as say a certain slang expression or engage in erotic self-stimulation. Instead of asking for a promise, ask one to make a decision to change and to renew his commitment to himself or herself each day.

From time to time, a husband and wife can give their sexual love sparkle by exchanging written and spoken descriptions of romantic experiences that they would like to have in marriage. I often hear the phrase "Good health adds years to your life, but keep in mind that it is equally true that love adds life to your years."

DIFFERENCES IN DESIRE

There are many marriages in which one individual thinks, "tonight is the night," but his or her partner does not agree. One is hot when the other is not. I counseled with a couple who had a wide difference as to sexual desire. In this case, the wife told me she would like sex nearly every day, but her husband seemed to be interested only two or three times a month.

What is considered to be normal? Many newlyweds relate sexually almost on a daily basis, and older couples and those with health problems may get together very seldom. The majority of couples, ages twenty to forty-five, in one study reported that they engage in sexual intercourse two or three times a week. The typical sexual frequency can be described as follows: Newlyweds—Tri weekly, midlife couples—Try weekly, and older couples—Try weakly.

Sex, like hunger, seeks periodic satisfaction, but it is more complicated to satisfy oneself and one's partner sexually than it is to satisfy one's appetite for food.

Some women have an increased desire for sex as they get older. One reason for this is the female body increases its production of testosterone with age. Testosterone is the hormone that engenders libido, or sexual desire. In contrast, men's bodies produce less testosterone as they get older. This hormonal difference can help close the "desire gap" for some couples. The following humorous case exemplifies an extreme difference in desire.

> Dear Abby:
> I am 44 and Louie (my husband) is 49. I work in a laundry ten hours a day. When night comes I need a rest. Louie still acts like a teen-ager when it comes to sex. He can't get enough.
> On weekends if we go for a drive in the country, Louie starts looking for an abandoned farmhouse or a secluded road. When we go for a walk in the woods, Louie looks for some bushes for us to crawl under. (We were nearly caught several times.)
> I got so tired of being hounded for sex; I made Louie ask our family doctor how much sex was normal for people our age. The doctor said three times a week was normal, so now Louie keeps a record. If it's less than three times a week, he says I owe him, and he adds it onto the next week.
> I am falling behind, and dread the thought of going on a vacation trip with this man. Any suggestions?
> Tired

Louie's compulsive quest for more and more sex suggests a need for psychotherapy or marriage therapy. He may be turning to the "marriage bed" in a futile effort to allay anxiety. However, this man's excessive sexual appetite is more likely to be diminished by marriage counseling than mental health treatment. This couple seems to have a "demanding-detaching" syndrome going. This means the more erotic moves he makes toward her, the more she tries to detach herself from him. But the more often she withdraws, the more energetically he pursues. A capable marriage therapist can help this couple end their frustrating circle by convincing the wife to become more sexually assertive. If the counselor can succeed in getting the wife to take the initiative more often, the husband in many cases will relax and stop demanding so much. This wife may think that if she begins to pursue her husband, he will want sex all the more; but usually just the opposite is true. At the same time, the therapist needs to persuade the husband to diminish his effort. There are also many marriages in which the wife is sexually demanding and the husband is detaching.

When a husband and wife have a desire discrepancy, I generally recommend that the one having a lower libido—sex drive—make a decision to more often cooperate with the partner having greater desire and to begin initiating sexual love. Doing this can escalate positive feelings and revitalize love. In a loving marriage, sex is an act of love.

To rekindle the sexual love in your marriage, you and your partner must have a desire to create a desire.

A Marriage and Sex Therapist Writes about Intimacy in Her Own Marriage

In her book *The Sex-Starved Marriage,* Michele Weiner-Davis writes about how her relationship with her husband Jim blossomed after they got their sexual love back on track. She explained

> Once Jim recognized that I truly understood his hurt, his sense of rejection, and his desire to be close to me sexually, and once he saw that I was devoted to bringing back the passion in our lives, something within him changed. Like all other couples, our lives are hectic, and there are lots of times when we get sexually out of sync. But now, rather than feel hurt, rejected, or angry, he knows that just happens sometimes. Plus, he feels confident that if he "needs" me, I'm never too far away. That's important to me. The rewards I've received for loving him in this way have been immeasurable. He's

been a happy man. After nearly three decades together, our marriage has never been stronger. We are like two giddy newlyweds, and we've been this way for so long. We talk, we laugh, we share, and we make love. Bridging the desire gap isn't about having more or less sex; it's about loving each other.

I tell you this because I can easily recall those dark times early on when our sexual differences divided us. I'm certain you've had dark times of your own. But I want you to know that no matter how distant you and your spouse may feel, it's never too late to have a loving, intimate, mutually satisfying sexual relationship. *Never*. It's never too late to rediscover the pleasures of sex and the bond that comes from being in sync sexually.[5]

Michele expressed these additional words of wisdom about marital intimacy.

"In addition to the closeness a man feels to his wife, a solid sexual relationship does wonders for his self-esteem and sense of masculinity. Little corrodes a man's feeling of confidence and sense of virility more than his wife's continual rejections."[6]

In a letter to Dr. Laura Schlessinger, one woman wrote,

My marriage has gotten so incredibly good over the last two years thanks to my following your advice. . . . You said a wife should not tell her husband no when he wants to have sex with her. I thought it couldn't hurt to give it a try. Well let me tell you it has made a huge difference in my life. What I saw as a daunting task has actually made my life easier. Because I am now saying yes instead of no, I have a man who wants to be with me instead of anywhere else.[7]

Dr. Laura's advice turned a good husband into an amazing one, and it turned this immature girl into a loving wife, better mother, and better human being.

Not Being in the Mood

At times, one partner may be more in the mood for sex than the other; however, not being in the mood is insufficient reason for declining. There is probably no better way to get in the mood than to proceed with the act itself. There will be times when one partner is extremely fatigued. This calls for understanding and acceptance on the part of the other, yet being moderately tired is hardly sufficient reason for refusal.

PRIME TIME

We enjoy any experience more, including sex, if we are rested and feeling good when we participate in it. Our employment would be drudgery if we always went to work after a long day or night of exhausting activities.

Likewise, sex may become a chore for a couple who participate in it usually when they are exhausted. A couple can enrich their sex life by giving it high enough priority for it to occasionally preempt other activities. They would be wise to often arrange a "sex date" with each other and rendezvous at home or at a hotel or vacation resort.

SEXUAL DYSFUNCTIONS

Professors Corydon Hammond and Robert Stahmann report that several studies have shown that even happily married couples can have sexual dysfunctions. They cite research information recorded in the New England Journal of Medicine, which revealed that 83 percent of couples not in therapy rated their marriages as "happy" or "very happy." Even though most of these couples had happy marriages, 40 percent of the husbands and 63 percent of the wives acknowledged having a sexual dysfunction.[8]

This information shows that a happy marriage will not magically cause a sexual problem to fade away. This chapter has been written to help couples avoid and resolve sexual dissatisfaction. Reading will enable some couples to achieve this; however, various other married couples might also need marriage counseling and sex therapy to attain mutual sexual satisfaction. If so, they *must* find a marriage and family therapist or some other professional who is capable of helping them progress in this important dimension of their marriage.

Here is a complaint from a sexually disappointed wife: "I've tried. I've worn everything from sexy negligees to nothing at all. All my guy does is turn his head and say, 'Move, you're in my way. I can't see the TV' or 'Put some clothes on; you're going to catch cold.' And here is a complaint from a sexually disappointed husband: "On our wedding night my bride said, 'it's been such a beautiful day;

let's not spoil it with sex.' She gave me no hint while I courted her that she felt that way about sex."

The desires that a husband and wife have about what to do for a vacation together influence their marriage only once or twice a year. Their attitudes about presidential candidates influence their relationship only once every four years. In contrast, attitudes and feelings about love and sex influence a couple's relationship every day of the year.

You can choose to repeatedly rejoice about the fact that you have each other and you can decide and redecide to rekindle your romantic and sexual love in your marriage. It is important that you decide to have enthusiasm about eroticism with your marriage partner. Being erotic together as well as romantic can regularly revitalize your love and even protect it against divorce.

SEXUAL DIFFERENCES BETWEEN HUSBAND AND WIFE

The orgasm for men and women is more alike than different. In both sexes, it can be described as a buildup of muscle tension and an escalation of nerve ending sensations until there is a physiological explosion of contractions and sensations. There are two differences, however, between men and women. For a man, the sexual climax is more directly a reproductive act than it is for a woman. Men ejaculate semen having hundreds of millions of sperm cells at the time of orgasm. In contrast, women do not necessarily ovulate at the time of orgasm. The other gender difference is women's ability to experience multiple orgasms while most men can climax only once during each episode of lovemaking.

HAVE NO PERFORMANCE GOALS

Having sexual performance goals results in psychological "spectatoring" of oneself during lovemaking. This critical eye that one keeps on himself or herself generates anxiety and reduces the joy of sex. If one has performance goals he or she may have anxiety about reaching these goals. Goals in lovemaking tend to backfire. If a couple's lovemaking goal is always sexual intercourse or if their goal is simultaneous orgasm or if they have any other sexual goals, they are less likely to enjoy sex. Anxiety, which is a form of fear, takes priority over one's sexual emotions. Fear of anything prepares the body for fight or flight. It does not prepare the body for sex. A couple will enjoy sex more and with less dysfunction if they focus on enjoying their five senses instead of trying to reach certain goals. Sex should be a treat to all of the senses.

Among the most happily married couples, many do not experience simultaneous orgasm. Some say they do not like to climax simultaneously with the partner because it detracts from the quality of their individual experience. A number of authorities state that it is helpful if the woman climaxes moments before her husband. A husband can usually climax very soon after his wife has begun her orgasm. Among most young couples, a husband is inclined to climax before his wife does. Pertaining to arousal and progress toward climax, he often finds himself leaving third base and heading for home plate when his wife is just arriving at first base. This is undesirable because soon after a husband achieves orgasm, he looses erection. Subsequently, there is little more that he can do with his penis in an effort to help satisfy his wife. However, a loving husband will continue to caress his wife erotically until she is satisfied.

In the sexual relationship, what frustrates many young couples is the husband coming to orgasm quickly and the wife slowly or not at all. Each can do something mentally to remedy this situation. Some husbands seem to have a "wham, bam, thank you ma'am," style of lovemaking. Emerson said, "Anger slowly, there's plenty of time." Likewise, a man needs to say to himself, "Make love slowly, there is plenty of time." When a couple explains to me that the sexual pattern in their relationship is characterized by her just barely becoming sexually aroused when he is nearing climax, I sometimes ask the woman what she thinks about during sex. In some cases, the wife tells me, she thinks about Susan's dental appointment, Jimmy's little league game, the unpaid bills, and the paint that the ceiling needs. I have found if I can get these women to remember to think about sex during sex, they enjoy it more and are more likely to progress toward orgasm.

An individual may find it difficult to respond sexually, even though the desire may be there, when he or she is in a state of illness or extreme fatigue or is emotionally upset about something. Don't expect your partner to experience orgasm every time you make love. Occasionally your marriage partner might be unable to experience orgasm or may prefer not to. If so, do not worry about it. However, if one habitually shows a lack of enthusiasm and seldom has a desire to experience an orgasm, this can be so disappointing to the partner that it can hurt the relationship.

Feminine Response

Women who have a low orgasm threshold are able to arrive at climax with very little stimulation. But women who have a high orgasm threshold require considerable clitoral caressing in order to reach sexual climax. The high-threshold woman is likely to have a more satisfying experience if she and her husband prolong their sex play until she is highly aroused before they proceed with coitus—sexual intercourse.

Husbands and wives can take physical action to modify the timing of their sexual response for the purpose of his slowing down and her speeding up. Men ejaculating quickly and women climaxing slowly or not at all frustrates and disappoints many couples. Because of this disappointment, some husbands and wives give up sex indefinitely and hope something like magic will happen to improve things. A capable sex therapist will have the knowledge and ability to help a couple cope with this circumstance by teaching them a certain procedure.

The procedure includes four stages and requires only four weeks, more or less. The first stage involves love play to the point of orgasm for the husband, and for the wife if she wishes, but it precludes actual sexual intercourse. Vaginal sex is prohibited the first week because it is too stimulating for the husband. The major focus of sex play must be on the husband, with the wife caressing his genitals while he tunes in to his pre-ejaculatory nerve ending sensations. When he is near climax, he signals to his wife, and she stops her caressing. When it is "safe," he advises her, and she continues but stops when he again informs her that he is near. By the fourth time, he allows himself to ejaculate. This nonvaginal sex should be engaged in several times during the first week. The second, third, and fourth weeks also entail a process of stopping and starting, but sex is vaginal.

During the second stage, the wife is to take the above position, and when her husband nears orgasm, she temporarily withdraws and waits briefly until he tells her to continue in this start-stop process. Again, the fourth time, he allows himself to ejaculate. This time intravaginally. The side position is recommended for the third week, and the man in the above position during the fourth week. The same start-stop procedure is used in stages three and four as in the first two. By using this method, over 95 percent of couples succeed in slowing down the ejaculatory response. A couple might need to repeat this every once in a while.

Women can heighten their pleasure and speed up their response by regularly doing the Kegel exercise, named after the physician Arnold Kegel. This can be done by quickly tightening and relaxing the vagina about ten times and by slowly tightening and relaxing the vagina about ten more times—like ten quick winks and then ten slow ones. This is to be done three times a day while standing, sitting, or lying down. This apparently amplifies sexual pleasure by improving muscle tone and activating nerve endings that are deeply embedded in the pubococcygeal vaginal muscle. Physicians and nurses also teach women this exercise in childbirth educational programs to help pregnant women prepare for delivery.

Although a woman may experience greater sexual satisfaction after only a few weeks of exercising, she would probably do well to continue doing them for a lifetime or as long as she is sexually active. While the Kegel exercise can help improve sexual love for many women, a certain number of women also need to do this routine regularly to improve urinary control.

ERECTION DYSFUNCTION

From 40 to 50 percent of erection problems may result from physical factors such as diabetes and drugs, including alcohol, smoking tobacco, marijuana, and certain prescriptions. As with most other sexual difficulties, impotence may be caused by a lack of information, by misinformation, by marital conflict, or by emotional stress. If a husband thinks his difficulty in achieving an erection is physically induced, he needs to know that if he often awakens with an erection, this is evidence that he is probably OK physically.

Medication for a chronic health condition, such as hypertension or depression, can lower libido and circumvent erection and ejaculation ability. Thus, whenever possible, one would do well to use alternatives to medication. These alternatives include such things as the following: nutrition changes, exercising regularly, and relaxation. Viagra and other similar prescription medications may be a useful way of dealing with erection problems. Other medical interventions are also available. Medically prescribed mechanical aids and surgery are also possibilities.

A CASE OF IMPOTENCE

Erectile dysfunction is widely treated with medical intervention by the use of medication and other methods.

Dr. David R. Mace, internationally acclaimed marriage consultant, successfully treated a case of impotence of five years' duration. Success was achieved with this couple mainly by getting them to give up their performance goals.

Impotence refers to inability to engage in sexual intercourse because of being unable to acquire and maintain an erection. Early in marriage, this husband had been potent and his wife had been highly responsive sexually. The husband eventually became impotent due to sexual performance goals that both of them had in mind for him. In search of help, the husband first went to the family physician, then to a urologist. Weekly prostate massage and later testosterone shots were tried without success. As time went on, the husband and wife were both very disappointed and upset. The marriage grew worse and worse, and eventually the husband sought treatment from another physician who referred him at once to a psychotherapist.

After two years of psychotherapy, the husband was still impotent and the marriage was in serious trouble. Then came a breakthrough. The wife read a magazine article about sex therapy. Inquiry was made, and the couple was referred to Dr. David Mace. In five years of treatment, no physician or therapist had ever involved the wife. Dr. Mace asked the wife to come for counseling with her husband and determined that performance goals were the main cause of the sexual dysfunction, so he took away their goal of the husband being potent during sexual intercourse by telling them they were not to attempt it for the time being. He instructed them in sensate focus and noncoital sex. Sensate focus refers to focusing on the pleasure of the senses during lovemaking and noncoital sex includes all aspects of erotic lovemaking except sexual intercourse. It may lead to orgasm for one or both.

Only two weeks later, in their second interview, the couple reported success. By sensate focus and noncoital sex, the husband had acquired an erection and both had climaxed. Later during this kind of lovemaking, the wife said to her husband: "Do you think that if we were allowed to go further, you could maintain your erection?" and immediately he lost it. Dr. Mace said she had again brought in the performance demand. So when he got them together, he talked to them very firmly about "the performance demand," and then he told them to continue as before, still no intercourse.

At the time of the fourth interview, David Mace gave them permission to proceed with intercourse, something that had not happened for a long, long time for this couple; but he told them the time was not ready for ejaculation to occur within the vagina. The couple arrived for their fifth interview looking very happy, and the husband said to Dr. Mace, "I have a confession to make. We put the penis in the vagina, and I was able to continue having an erection, and I remembered that ejaculation was not to occur within the vagina, but I thought 'Oh, well, why not?' and went right ahead. Are you angry? You don't look angry." Dr. Mace assured the husband that he was not angry but was very glad about the husband's success, and he said to him: "Why did I tell you not to ejaculate in the vagina? Because your whole problem was . . . you had the feeling, 'I've got to do it; I've got to do it.'" David Mace reversed this by getting the husband to think, "I mustn't do it; I mustn't do it."

Summarizing the case, Dr. Mace said, "Eight months later, I saw this couple and visited with them . . . and they told me that everything was okay. So in the course of nine hours of counseling, we cleared up a problem that had burdened and distressed these two people and almost broken their marriage over a five-year period."[9]

YOUR SEXUAL MACHINERY

If a woman has dysparunia—that is, pain during sex—or vaginismus, or involuntary vaginal spasm, first she should talk with and be examined by her OB-GYN. If a man has ED—erection dysfunction—or difficulty ejaculating, he should talk with and be examined by his urologist. Medications often interfere with the functioning of a man's sexual machinery. For example, various antidepressants might interfere with a man's ability to ejaculate. As men get older, their physical health conditions more often interfere with their ability to function sexually than when women get older. Many women, as they get older, are more sexually responsive, and many have learned how to experience multiple orgasms during one episode of lovemaking. It is important that you check things out physically and not just assume that your sexual difficulties are psychosomatic.

OUCH

A newlywed couple came to me for counseling because sex was a painful experience for the wife. Our dialogue went something like this:

C.S.: Are you using a lubricant?

Client: No, we have never used a lubricant because we have read that if a woman is really interested in sex she will produce adequate vaginal lubrication at the time of lovemaking.

C.S.: Some women don't produce enough lubrication even though there is love for the husband and an interest in sex. Would you be willing to try a lubricant?

Client: Yes, we would.

This couple reported back to me that with the use of a small amount of lubricant applied vaginally prior to sexual love, there was no more pain and the wife was able to enjoy sex for the first time in their marriage.

When a lubricant is necessary, it is very important that a sterilized lubricant, such as Astro Glide or KY Jelly, be used. Lubricants that are unsterilized, such as Vaseline and hand lotions, may result in urinary tract infection.

Another contributor to infections is the habitual use of a vaginal douche, which is not only unnecessary for cleanliness but also disrupts the natural biochemistry of the vagina. Regular douching might make the vagina more vulnerable to infection.

If a woman drinks sufficient liquids every day and if she and her husband are careful to practice principles of cleanliness, they are more likely to have good health. However, no matter how much care is taken, some women have repeated flare-ups of urinary tract infections. In such a case, a physician may be able to prescribe medication to be taken regularly to prevent this nuisance.

ABSTINENCE: WHEN?

Unnecessary abstinence from sex does not build a husband's or wife's character, and long intervals between times do not necessarily increase the pleasure or the quality of the experience. Yet, there are times when abstinence is either necessary or desirable. If a couple is using the rhythm method of family planning, they will need to abstain for approximately eight days of each menstrual cycle, during the wife's most fertile time. Also, many couples choose to abstain during menstruation. During pregnancy, most couples can continue to be sexually active, but they should confer with their physician about this because every woman's pregnancies and state of health are unique.

Even though a couple may choose to abstain from actual intercourse during a certain time, it is not necessary that they abstain from sexual lovemaking. Some couples will find lovemaking during these times not only acceptable, but also a valuable strength to their relationship. On those occasions when a husband and wife would choose not to go "all the way," they can still do a lot of touching and creative cuddling.

Menopause usually begins in a woman's forties, and after it is complete, she can no longer become pregnant. Nevertheless, she can still enjoy sex to the fullest and can experience orgasm after menopause as well as before. In fact, some wives report enjoying sex considerably more after menopause because they are confident they cannot become pregnant.

SEXUAL COMMUNICATION INVENTORY

	Yes	No	Sometimes	Usually	Seldom
1. Does your partner clearly explain matters related to sexual love?					
2. Do you let your partner know what turns you off sexually?					
3. Do you feel guilty over any previous sexual relationships?					
4. Is it easier to discuss sex with someone other than your partner?					
5. Do you and your partner know each other's thoughts about contraception?					
6. Do you find it difficult to ask your partner to engage in sexual activity?					
7. Do you and your partner discuss ways to improve your sexual relationship?					
8. Do you and your partner disagree over how often you want to engage in sexual love?					

	Yes	No	Sometimes	Usually	Seldom
9. Do you think your partner understands your sexual desires?					
10. Does your partner complain that you do not understand his/her sexual wishes?					
11. Do you avoid discussing with your partner any aspects of your sexual experiences?					
12. Does your partner make sexual desires known to you?					
13. While engaging in sexual lovemaking, do you and your partner talk to each other?					
14. Do you and your partner discuss the matter of variety in your sexual experiences with each other?					
15. Are you and your partner physically affectionate with each other?					
16. Do you and your partner express affection with words and touch?					

Sexual Satisfaction Indicator

Yourself	Satisfied	Dissatisfied
Our overall daily affection		
Our ability to openly discuss sexual intimacy		
The time of day when we usually make love		
Our way of initiating sexual intimacy		
The setting and atmosphere		
Amount of love play		
Nature and variety of love play		
Our timing during the act of lovemaking		
Our frequency		
Overall satisfaction		
Your Marriage Partner	**Satisfied**	**Dissatisfied**
Our overall daily affection		
Our ability to openly discuss sexual intimacy		
The time of day when we usually make love		
Our way of initiating sexual intimacy		
The setting and atmosphere		
Amount of love play		
Nature and variety of love play		
Our timing during the act of lovemaking		
Our frequency		
Overall satisfaction		

STATEMENTS CONCERNING SEXUAL LOVE FOR HUSBANDS AND WIVES TO DISCUSS

1. The relationship between love and sex in our marriage is

   _____

2. Marriage without sex would be _____

3. Ways in which sex has become of greater or lesser importance in our marriage are

   _____

4. I feel most comfortable with you when

   _____

5. What appeals to me sexually is _____

6. My thoughts about family planning are

   _____

7. Decisions about family planning should be made by

   _____

8. Sexual satisfaction contributes to marital happiness because _____

9. Factors that help or hinder the quality of our sexual relationship are _____

10. The interaction of health and sex in our marriage is

    _____

11. A marriage partner's sexual responsibility is to

    _____

12. The role of orgasm in sexual enjoyment is

    _____

13. Ways in which one's sexual feelings, desire, and arousal are influenced by the behavior of a husband or wife:

    _____

14. The importance of
    a. cleanliness and grooming: _____
    b. seclusion and privacy without the possibility of interruption: _____

15. Mutually satisfying sex could strengthen a rickety marriage by

    _____

16. My thoughts on

    c. prime time: _____ a.m. vs. p.m.

    d. lighting and lovemaking: _____

17. Thoughts affect sexual interest and response by

_____

18. Pleasure and satisfaction are enhanced by planning and communicating rather than by relying entirely on spontaneous desire: _____

19. I wish that _____

NOTES

1. Michele Weiner-Davis, *The Sex-Starved Marriage* (New York: Simon & Schuster), 8.

2. Proverbs 5:18–19.

3. Helen Singer Kaplan, MD, PhD, *The New Sex Therapy* (New York: Brunner/Mazel, 1974), 14.

4. Charlie Shedd, *Letters to Karen* (New York: Avon, 1967), 111.

5. Weiner-Davis, *The Sex-Starved Marriage*, 57.

6. Ibid.

7. Copyright© 2010 by Take On the Day, LLC. Reprinted by permission.

8. Brent A. Barlow, *What Husbands Expect of Wives* (Salt Lake City: Deseret Book, 1983), 63.

9. Dr. David Mace. Lecture notes in author's possession.

Chart on pp. 108–109 authored by Millard J. Bienvenu. Revised by Clark Swain, PhD, marriage, family, and individual counselor.

12

Controlling Anger in
Your Marriage

MISMANAGEMENT OF ANGER

The mismanagement of anger is one of the main causes of misery and failure in marriages today.

Anger is an emotion that each of us feels rise within us from time to time. We are likely to feel anger toward a marriage partner or anyone who repeatedly says and does things that frustrate us, annoy us, or hurt our feelings. Anger is often a secondary emotion that results from hurt feelings. Although anger is a normal emotion, if it is expressed explosively, it can do physical, emotional, and spiritual harm. We now know that the hostile personality is more vulnerable to heart disease than the hyperactive "Type A" personality. Intense anger raises blood pressure, heart rate, and the amount of fatty acid in the bloodstream. The habit of strong anger or the habit of retaining a resentful and hostile attitude increases the possibility of hypertension, migraine headaches, ulcers, heart disease, and strokes.

Our love relationships and friendships will deteriorate if we do not manage our anger intelligently.

BRIDLING OUR ANGER

A scripture tells us, "Bridle all your passions, that ye may be filled with love."[1] *Passion* refers to our emotions. We must especially bridle the emotion of anger. Anger is an emotion that we must rein in, just as we use the reins of a bridle to control a horse we are riding.

EXPRESSIONS OF ANGER

Anger that is fast, strong, or long will harm the happiness of a marriage or any relationship.

There are three expressions of anger that are especially harmful. I call these hand grenade anger; volcano anger; and slow-burn, smoldering anger, which is hostility kept simmering in one's mind.

When we hand grenade our anger, we throw it out as soon as we feel it. Although this might momentarily relieve us of some tension, it offends and engenders retaliation. A clash of words and onrush of action bruises feelings and injures goodwill. People who quickly hurl out a grenade of anger need to learn to respond slowly when becoming angry. Usually when a husband and wife say, "We had a fight," they really mean they had a war of words, not a physical fight.

We tend to erupt volcanically with an angry outburst after we have repeatedly postponed communicating that we are feeling frustrated, annoyed, or hurt about something someone is doing or not doing. We're better off promptly resolving an annoyance with a mild skirmish than waiting until our anger has escalated to a point of eruptive intensity. What may have been only a tremor in the relationship may eventually erupt into a volcanic blast unless it is settled promptly. Because of its magnitude, volcanic anger can be as devastating to relationships as hand grenade anger, even though it is expressed less often.

Slow-burn, smoldering anger characterizes those individuals who are passively hostile. They seldom explode or erupt, but they retain resentment and hold grudges. They've never learned that forgiving is loving and that it is a gift the offended one gives to himself as well as to the one whom he is forgiving. Slow-burn, smoldering anger is insidiously expressed in oblique, indirect ways such as sarcasm, the silent treatment, and stubbornness.

By following three steps recommended by Dr. David R. Mace, we can more often avoid the destructive expressions of hand grenade, volcanic, and slow-burn anger.

> It might help us to remember to do these three things if we think of the key word ARE: A, Admit it; R, Restrain it, and E, Explain it.
>
> These steps are: First, when we are chronically annoyed about someone's behavior we must have the courage to tactfully admit our displeasure to him or her. A clear request is far less likely to wound feelings of love than a cutting comment or a sudden burst of rage. Acknowledging our anger is also better than sulking.
>
> Second, while communicating our anger we must restrain it, and not let it get out of hand. Anger threatens any love relationship, so it must be controlled as soon as possible.
>
> Third, it is imperative that we explain why we became angry. We need to make statements such as, "It hurts my feelings when you . . ." "I'm annoyed about your . . ." "I feel irritated because . . ." It upsets me when . . ." "I wish you would . . ." Only then can our marriage partner (or family member, or friend) know how to avoid offending us in the same way in the future. When we receive this kind of message, we may need to improve. Commenting to your marriage partner "I'm sorry, I apologize," is important for helping in restoring friendly feelings. A stubborn refusal to make personal improvements dooms a relationship to mediocrity. For a happy marriage, then, we must learn to manage our anger by calmly admitting to our partner that we are getting angry, by restraining our hostile feelings, and by explaining to our husband or wife exactly what caused the angry feelings to develop.[2]

Pop psychology has influenced many people, including certain mental health professionals, to erroneously think that the best way to get rid of a negative feeling is to express that feeling strongly. Just the opposite is true. Any feeling that is expressed strongly is reinforced. An emotion, like fire, requires fuel to keep going. The emotion of anger, like any other emotion, becomes stronger when "fuel" is added. Raising one's voice, saying mean things, throwing things, and striking the person one feels the anger toward are actions that add fuel to the flames of one's anger. Research findings show the more strongly family members "bad mouth" each other with angry words, the more likely they will physically attack each other. Showing hostility in an angry tone of voice strengthens the feeling of hostility. On the other hand, communicating love to anyone tends to increase our feelings of love for that person. Expressing any emotion magnifies the intensity of the emotion.

In a shouting match, agreements cannot be reached because neither partner listens to the other. If you lower your voice, your marriage partner will probably do the same. I know a couple who uses self-imposed social pressure to help them speak in composed voices when angry. When they strongly disagree, they go to a pleasant restaurant to talk calmly and eat.

CONTROLLING ANGER

It is necessary at times to express anger, but we need to do it in a calm, controlled manner. Studies reveal that the possibility of physical violence goes up in direct proportion to rude and angry words.

In one study, 80 percent of the couples who were explosive with their words became physically abusive.

Anger is a fire that burns with more fury whenever we add more fuel. Adding wood to a fire heightens the heat; likewise, fueling anger with angry thoughts, words, and actions heightens the intensity of one's anger.

If anger becomes intense, maintain distance to avoid physical confrontation.

- Take time out. Get away from each other.
- Plan to communicate soon after both of you have calmed down.
- Keep discussion simple and short. The issue does not have to be settled today or tonight.
- Release angry feelings through physical exercise—take a walk, do yard work, hit golf balls.
- Never brag about your anger and don't be ashamed of it; just overcome it as soon as you can.
- Have an attitude of forgiveness. We need to forgive for our own health and happiness.

Time Out for Couples and Families

Temporarily Get Away from Each Other[3]

When I realize that my anger or the anger of my marriage partner or any other family member is getting out of control, I will request a time out and leave at once. I will not hit or kick anything, and I will not slam the door.

I will be gone no longer than two hours. I will take a walk or use up the anger energy in some other way. I will avoid focusing on resentments. When I return, I will check to find out if my marriage partner or other family member is ready to resume discussion. If not, we will agree on a specific time to reexamine the conflict. (I'll start the conversation with, "I know that I was partly wrong and partly right." I will then acknowledge any mistakes I made.)

If my marriage partner or family member requests a time out and walks away, I will agree to this, and I will let her or him go without a hassle, no matter what is going on. I will avoid focusing on resentments. When he or she returns, we will set a specific time for reexamining the conflict. (I will start the conversation with, "I know that I was partly wrong and partly right." I will then acknowledge any mistakes I made.)

Name: _____   Date: _____

Name: _____   Date: _____

One remains calm. It will help if you and your mate do not get angry at the same time. If you can remain calm when your partner becomes angry, anger will not cause your relationship to deteriorate into a downward spiral. If you are both getting mad, get away from each other for a short time. The clergyman who performed our wedding ceremony cautioned, "Whenever you feel like arguing, take a walk outdoors in opposite directions. If you will do this, you will both get a lot of fresh air and will become great outdoorsmen." A brisk walk can provide the necessary exercise to help alter our emotional state. It can give us time to think clearly and will lessen the likelihood that our words and actions will be cause for regret.

Being apart during acute anger is a safety precaution as well as a tension reliever.

When you and your spouse become angry at each other at bedtime, it might be a good idea, *occasionally*, for one of you to go into another bedroom to sleep. If you don't have an extra bedroom, go into the living room and try sleeping on the couch. Making it a practice to get away from each other during times of intense anger can save wear and tear all your marriage.

If you and your partner find that anger interferes with your efforts to iron out the wrinkles in your relationship, temporarily stop trying to reach an agreement by talking it out face to face. Instead, try getting your point across by letters and phone calls. An advantage of writing an angry message, over speaking it, lies in having the chance to read and reconsider your words. One man said in a letter to his wife, "I want to write you this note because I think I can write more in a few sentences than I can say in an hour. . . . When we talk about these things too often we just talk in circles." Writing and phoning provide the respective safety features of time and space.

REMEMBER TO FORGET

As I was leaving for work one day, my wife and I exchanged some angry words. As I left she said, "It will be a long time before I feel like loving you again!" When I arrived home from work, I edged into the house defensively, expecting trouble. When she saw me, she cheerfully said, "Hi." I was surprised and said, "Hey, aren't you mad at me?" "What about?" she asked. She had forgotten, or at least had disregarded, our anger. In some cases, an individual remembers in detail and even memorizes the angry words a marriage partner has spoken. He begins to convince himself that his partner is mean and does not love him. Remember and reminisce about the pleasant times in your marriage and family, and forget the unpleasant times.

MAKING AMENDS

I have had good control over my anger for many years because of making a conscious effort. Once in a while, however, I slip and speak with quick unkindness to my wife. When this happens, I have learned that the words "I'm sorry, I apologize" work like magic in restoring good feelings. I know that if my apology is to be accepted, I must truly feel sorry and I must convey this feeling by the tone of my voice. A hug or a pat on the shoulder and an additional statement, such as "I love you, and I hope you will forgive me," can help heal hurt feelings.

FORGIVING

Lloyd Newell said,

> Every relationship—between family members, neighbors, and friends—is made up of imperfect people, ourselves included. Slights and misunderstanding are inevitable. When we hold on to our anger, we may think we're exacting justice from our offender, but in reality we are punishing ourselves. When we forgive, we aren't minimizing the injury—we're allowing it to heal. When we admit our own errors and seek forgiveness ourselves, we aren't excusing the errors others may have made—we're simply opening the door to compassion and peace.[4]

IT'S BETTER TO DWELL IN THE WILDERNESS

No happily married couple would deliberately set out to wreck their marriage, yet many couples do ruin their marriages by mismanaging their anger. Anger comes occasionally to every marriage, but it does not have to be destructive. Anger can be a friend in disguise by showing each partner what needs to be done to improve their relationship. The important thing is what we say and do when we are angry. The habit of contention must be avoided in marriage, as in any other human relationship, if marriage is to be satisfying. Proverbs 21:19 says, "Tis better to dwell in the wilderness than to live with a contentious and angry woman." Likewise, we can say it might be better for a woman to dwell in the wilderness than to live with a contentious and angry man.

Accept anger that continually develops in your marriage and family as a sign that there is a need to improve behavior and relationships. You and your partner can learn to communicate anger safely and work together to overcome it.

A considerable number of people seem to think that their anger problem is inherited. One woman said, "I'm German, so I have a bad temper." Other people have made statements such as "She's a redhead and has a fiery disposition" or "He's a feisty Irishman." Although heredity influences personality, the habit of communicating with anger is developed through a lack of effort to control one's anger. The pattern of stormy behavior can be overcome like any other bad habit. Behavioral and mental health counseling can help in many cases. Certain medications can help some people control anger and other negative emotions such as anxiety and depression.

QUOTATIONS TO HELP CONTROL ANGER

Memorizing or regularly reading quotations such as the following can help one control his or her anger.

"Anger blows out the lamp of the mind."
Robert G. Ingersoll, American Lawyer

"Anger and aggression are irrational and self-defeating."
Albert Ellis, psychologist

"Say Goodbye to Anger."
Wayne Dyer, psychologist and author of Your Erroneous Zones

"He that is slow to anger is better than the mighty."
Proverbs 16:32

"A soft answer turneth away wrath: but grievous words stir up anger."
Proverbs 15:1

"Let every man be swift to hear, slow to speak, slow to anger. For the anger of man brings not to pass the righteousness of God."
James 1:19

"Anger slowly; there is plenty of time."
Ralph Waldo Emerson

"The real show of power is in restraint."
Aristotle

"Nothing cooks your goose faster than a boiling temper."
Anonymous

"A sharp tongue is one of the few edges that becomes sharper with use."
Anonymous

"Make no friendship with an angry man; and with a furious man thou shalt not go: lest thou learn his ways, and get a snare to thy soul."
Proverbs 22:24–25

"Stop being mean, bad-tempered and angry. Quarreling, harsh words, and dislike of others should have no place in your lives. Instead, be kind to each other, tenderhearted, forgiving one another."
Ephesians 4:31–32, Living New Testament

NOTES

1. Alma 38:12.
2. Talk on anger management given by Dr. David R. Mace at the Dallas Texas Marriage Conference, 1985. Notes in author's possession.
3. Adapted from M. McKay, PhD, P. Fanning, and K. Paleg, PhD, *Couple Skills: Making Your Relationship Work* (Oakland, CA: New Harbinger Publications, 1994), 169. Permission from Copyright Clearance Inc.
4. Lloyd D. Newell, *Music and the Spoken Word*, Program 4145, "Sweet Joy of Forgiveness," February 22, 2009.

13

Marriage: A Partnership with a

Need for Leadership

Fʀᴏᴍ ᴛʜᴇ ᴍᴀʀʀɪᴀɢᴇ counseling that I have done, I have become aware that even many couples who have been married for as long as ten or twenty years still have ineffective family government because of confusion as to who is chairman of the family board. In forming my thoughts for this chapter, I was unable to think of any organization where people function as a group that does not have a president, a chairman or chairwoman, or a leader of one kind or another. Can you imagine a civic council or a college department without a chairman or a director? No orchestra or band would function harmoniously without a director, even if all of its members were highly talented and capable musicians. Chaos and confusion would predominate if the trumpet players insisted on playing "Sempre Fidelis" while the violinists were playing "Brahms's Lullaby." Likewise, a family whose members have excellent individual ability may not be functioning well as a social unit if its members do not have a capable leader or if they refuse to follow leadership.

Tʜᴇʀᴇ Mᴜsᴛ Bᴇ Lᴇᴀᴅᴇʀsʜɪᴘ

Over the years, I have been employed as a farmhand, a construction worker, and a salesman. In all of these jobs, my bosses were men. As a university professor, all of my supervisors have been women. It makes no difference to me whether it is a man or a woman who is functioning as my leader. There must be leadership; therefore, I am willing to submit to it from persons of either sex. The department heads, under whose leadership I have worked, have each given me much freedom to make my own decisions and in a sense to "run my own show" as a marriage and family life educator and counselor. Likewise, even though our family accepts the New Testament teaching that the husband has the responsibility and challenge of being the leader in the home, my wife's decisions regarding home management are entirely her own. I do not intervene to tell her where to shop for groceries or what to buy except to tell her what I would like. Neither do I interfere in our home with her wishes for interior decoration, furniture arrangements, and general household management. We also granted our children freedom to make most of their own decisions. Children, of course, need parental guidance, and a family must make some decisions as a unit—this requires leadership.

A good leader of a family or any other group is not a dictator and, therefore, does not necessarily have things as he prefers them any more often than others have things as they prefer them. Let's suppose that a husband and wife disagree about something. It will save time if the husband quickly asserts himself, "I'm the leader and so we are going to do it my way." Such an unfair, self-centered approach may cost him his wife's goodwill even though she accepts him as head of the family. There is a better way. Usually they can negotiate and arrive at a mutually satisfying decision.

HOLY WEDLOCK OR UNHOLY DEADLOCK?

Let's suppose that Robert thinks he and Susan should buy a house, but she thinks they should rent. In this case, they can't merely agree to disagree. They must either buy or rent; and with this kind of difference, they cannot compromise by buying a house and living in it for a year and then renting another house the next year. Each can try to persuade the other to accept his or her way of thinking, but if neither succeeds in doing so, then one mate must be willing to yield to the wishes of the other.

Can a family always use a democratic majority vote in their decision making? Sometimes, but not always. Democracy means rule of the majority, and it is impossible to have a majority when there is only a husband and a wife. Also, there will be times when exactly one half of a family's members vote one way and the other half vote another way. Leadership is needed in even highly democratic families in order to loosen deadlocks and end stalemates.

Let's suppose that Robert and Lisa have four children, and all six members of the family are planning their summer vacation. Let's say that Robert and two of the children want to go to Canada, but Lisa and the other two children want to go to the Grand Canyon. Assuming that this family accepts the Judeo-Christian philosophy of family government, the husband will have the burden of leadership. If Robert is fair in his leadership role, he will be just as willing to go to the Grand Canyon as he is to Canada because one half of the members of the family want to go there.

In a family, it's important to talk things over and to consider each other's feelings and preferences. If every member of a family feels free to express himself or herself, and if each knows his or her ideas and wishes will be considered, there is more likely to be a feeling of "I win and you win" after certain decisions have been made.

Because of his research, Dr. John Gottman emphasizes the importance of husbands accepting influence from their wives.

YOU ARE NOT INFERIOR TO YOUR LEADER

Marriage can be thought of as a merger between the Robert Jones Corporation and the Lisa Smith Corporation, with Robert as president of the new company, Lisa as vice president, and their children as members of the board of directors. For those who may think that this is relegating the wife and children to an inferior position to that of the husband, I want to make it clear that I do not think that the leader of any country, organization, or group is superior to the citizens or members. A leader is not superior to the members of his group; he simply performs a different function, a different role. It is his job to synthesize the input of all family members. Women as well as men respect strong leaders, but none of us want to be ruled by a self-centered dictator.

Because of your respect for the leader of your marriage and family, you support him even when you do not agree with some of his ideas. You trust his wisdom to make appropriate decisions based on family input.

The Bible says the husband has the responsibility of leadership in the family, but it is clear that he is to lead with loving kindness. Here are some scriptures about this. See what you think of them.

During the New Testament era, Paul said,

"Wives, submit yourselves unto your own husbands, as unto the Lord. For the husband is the head of the wife, even as Christ is the head of the church. . . . Husbands love your wives, even as Christ also loved the church, and gave himself for it. . . . So ought men to love their wives as their own bodies. He that loves his wife loves himself."[1]

"Wives, be subject to your husbands, as is fitting in the Lord. Husbands, love your wives, and do not be harsh with them. Children, obey your parents in everything, for this pleases the Lord. Fathers, do not provoke your children, lest they become discouraged."[2]

In a letter to Dr. Laura, a pastor clarified the scriptural teachings about Christian leadership as follows:

> Nowhere in the Bible is a woman told to blindly submit to the will of her husband. In fact, the first act of submission is on the husband's part! The husband is to submit himself to Christ and the will of God. When he does this he is not setting himself up as master but rather as servant of the Lord. Only then is the wife to submit to the will of her husband—because the will of her husband will be obedience to the Lord. So the wife is not submitting to the husband, but to God
> A man is supposed to love his wife as Christ loves the church. That means that a husband is required to love, care for, nurture, protect, comfort, and even be willing to die for his wife. That is love.[3]

All kinds of families need leadership, whether it be a two-parent family, a one-parent family, or newlyweds. The family and all other social units will run more smoothly and be more stable if one of its members is accepted by the others as the leader. This is especially true when the leader is self-confident and knows how to combine kindness with firmness.

NOTES

1. Ephesians 5: 22, 23, 25, 28. King James Version.
2. Colossians 3:18–21. Revised Standard Version.
3. Laura Shlessinger, "A Man Should Be Respected in His Own Home," chapter 7 in *The Proper Care and Feeding of Husbands* (New York: Harper, 2004), 50.

PART III

Being Happily Married to Yourself

The Relevance of Mental Health to Marital Health

Principles of mental health and happiness are the theme of part three.

Accepting yourself just as you are today, while striving toward a better self, is essential for happiness. Only when you wholeheartedly accept yourself can you be happily married to yourself, and you must be happily married to yourself before you can be happily married to anyone else. You will learn from the ensuing chapters that your level of mental health will be determined more by your attitude and your ability to take charge of your emotions than by the circumstances of your life.

You will also learn that if you want your life to be different, you can make it different by making decisions and taking action. You create yourself and your world, to a great extent, by your choices. Loving and living better is an achievement that begins with a decision that you are free to make.

14

Marriage and Personal

Crisis Adjustment

Ilost most of my eyesight in October 1956, when I was 21, while living in Eastern Canada. My vision began to blur while I was attending a football game. Within hours, I could not see well enough to distinguish one person from another. My condition was diagnosed as optic neuritis. Six weeks later, I took a plane home to Utah, where I was hospitalized for ten days. Medical treatment brought no improvement in my ability to see. I was blind except for shadow vision. This means I could see like a swimmer sees while opening his eyes under water. At this point, I was not emotionally upset because I thought my blindness was only temporary.

My fiancé, Eleanor, and I, in our third year of courtship, continued our wedding plans. To my knowledge, she never seriously considered not marrying me because of my physical handicap, and we were married ten months after the onset of my blindness.

I was not unhappy during the early months of my blindness, but later, this changed—not because the blindness became more severe, but because my attitude changed. Upon learning from medical specialists that I would never regain my eyesight, I began telling myself how awful, how unfortunate, and how tragic this was. This "silent sentence self-talk" brought on an emotional state of depression. My experience supports the principle that it is not the event as much as our attitude toward the event that determines our emotional state.

The Justice Trap

I fell into "the justice trap," as explained in the book *Your Erroneous Zones,* by Dr. Wayne Dyer. I told myself how unfair it was that blindness came to me at the age of twenty-one. After fifty-four years of blindness, I have concluded that I was right—it is unfair. However, nobody has promised us that life on earth would be entirely fair. I grew up in a loving family, I live in a free country, and I've had the opportunity to get a college education, benefits denied to most of the world's population. Unfairness is part of the human condition.

Epictetus, a Greek slave who lived about two hundred years after Christ, taught that it is not the event itself that emotionally disturbs an individual, but one's judgment of or way of thinking about a negative event that upsets him. Beliefs or attitudes about the event determine one's emotional state more than the event itself. An event—interacting with the family's or individual's crisis-coping resources and with the perception of the event—may or may not produce a crisis.

Consider the following as resources that would likely help an individual cope with a crisis: having good health, being well educated, being vocationally trained, having a good income, having close friends, and having a devoted fiancé or marriage partner.

Throughout the early years of our marriage, my wife's lifestyle was essentially the same as it probably would have been had she married a man having no physical disability. I have always made an effort to be as independent as possible so that my wife can lead a "normal" life. We make an ongoing effort to be fair; Eleanor helps me with my profession, and I help her with the responsibilities of home and family life. On a daily basis, I help with household chores and, when they were young, with the care of our five children. I participate in these activities because I enjoy them and realize that nearly every day I will need my wife's assistance as a chauffeur, reader, or professional consultant.

I would not recommend that anyone go out and look for a marriage partner with a physical disability. The greater assistance that a handicapped individual will need from a mate can put a marriage under stress from time to time. But there are some benefits that the non-handicapped spouse can derive from this kind of marriage. There is the increased sharing of activities that can enhance companionship. A handicapped husband probably spends more time at home than most other husbands. For example, while other men are away from home attending a local ball game, I am usually home listening to the same game while I work in the kitchen. While other men are playing golf, I am probably home playing with our children.

TRIUMPHANT HILLS AND DISCOURAGING VALLEYS

Some knowledge of the psychodynamics of crisis adjustment can help individuals and family members adapt more quickly to a serious loss of any kind. In adjusting to a crisis, I believe most of us go through a roller-coaster pattern. The recovery and rising again of a "human roller coaster" after a crisis event is usually gradual and emotionally stressful. For most of us, our comeback is characterized by triumphant hills and discouraging valleys. Gradually and painfully, we regain our equilibrium. Eventually we can again find ourselves at the top of our "mountain." We have adjusted to our loss, and it no longer hurts. We have psychologically permitted our previous self to die and our new self to emerge.

Based on my experience, I believe that personal happiness contributes directly to marital happiness and vice versa. Again, one's judgment or definition of a crisis event contributes more to his emotional state than the event itself. I also believe that even though a physical disability or chronic illness can bring stress to a marriage, it can also bring certain benefits.

15

The Serenity to Accept the Things You Cannot Change

And the Courage to Change the Things You Can

A WELL-KNOWN MOTTO says, "God grant us the serenity to accept the things we cannot change, the courage to change the things we can change, and the wisdom to know the difference." If you have developed this kind of serenity and courage, you have two important planks in your platform of happiness. For happiness, each of us must learn to adjust. Adjustment means accepting the unchangeable and changing what can and should be changed.

If you are to be happy, you must surrender to being as you are. You must accept yourself as you are right now, because at this moment, you cannot be any different. If you want to be different, you can start changing tomorrow or even today, but for this moment, accept yourself just as you are.

If you are wondering whether or not you are an "OK person," your tendency might be to compare yourself with others. After comparing, you might conclude that you are inferior to some people and superior to others. The truth is, however, that you are not inferior or superior to anyone. Psychologist Maxwell Maltz says that an inferiority complex and a superiority complex are merely opposite sides of the same coin—and the coin is counterfeit. You cannot be inferior or superior to anyone; you are simply different. The famous essay "Desiderata" says, "If you compare yourself with others you may become vain and bitter; for always there will be greater and lesser persons than yourself."

Be Honest with Yourself

Full self-acceptance means that you accept the positives as well as the negatives about yourself. If your music teacher tells you and your friends that you sing beautifully, and you also believe you do, then accept this as one of your talents. Accept both your qualities and quirks. Make the most of what you have, and the least of what you don't have.

If you fully accept yourself, you will remain true to your beliefs and values, even on those occasions when the majority of people in your presence have different beliefs and values. Say what you believe if you believe it's true. Do what you believe, and believe in what you do.

If you truly accept yourself, you will live your life within the boundaries of your conscience. If you believe one way and behave a different way, you are being untrue to yourself, and for this you will feel guilty. Society does not make us feel guilty; we make ourselves feel guilty when we believe one way but act another way.

Finally, self-acceptance means being true to your likes and dislikes. For example, I like all kinds of music except hard rock. I especially like country music, which is what I heard most while growing up in Uintah Basin, Utah. Some may think it's undignified for a college professor to listen to country music, but I like it, and so I listen to it. Long ago I accepted this as a part of myself.

Be Honest with Life

Being honest with life, and being well-adjusted, means accepting things we cannot change and changing things that can and should be changed. It was not easy for me to accept the blindness that came to me at the age of twenty-one. However, as time went on, I realized that if I was to be happy I had to accept it, since there was nothing I could do to change the condition. Acceptance does not mean that we like something. It means that we are willing to go along with it and make the most of any situation.

Acceptance is one side of the coin of good adjustment and the other side is having the courage to change what we want to change, if it can be changed. After my blindness came on, I did quite a lot of hitchhiking. One time I was given a ride by a man who was a retired banker. His wife had died and their children had grown up and left home. He had always wanted to go to college, and here he was, enrolling as a freshman. He graduated three years later. He had the courage to change something he wanted to change—the courage to act.

Sometimes we just wish certain things were different instead of taking courageous action to change them. It has been said, "Never put your wishbone where your backbone ought to be." Yet many people make themselves miserable by playing an "if, wish, and should have" game, making statements like, "If I had enrolled in a junior college, I'd have better grades;" "I wish I had gotten a divorce before I got pregnant;" or "I should have chosen engineering for a career instead of education; then I'd have more money."

You must be happily married to yourself before you can be happily married to anyone else. Being happily married to yourself means that you wholeheartedly accept yourself as you are while making an ongoing effort to improve yourself. If we are to be happy, we must know how to adjust and then keep adjusting. Adjustment means having the serenity to accept the things we cannot change while having the courage to change the things we can.

16

Decision Making—A Key
to Success and Happiness

THE DECISIONS THAT we make and how we make them contribute to our success and happiness. Psychiatrist Eric Berne said, "The three words that we must learn to apply in living our lives if we are to be successful and happy are 'Yes,' 'No,' and 'Wow.' 'Yes' stands for whatever we decide in favor of; 'No' for what we decide against; and 'Wow' means that any decision that we make needs to be followed with enthusiastic action." For happiness, we don't have to have a lot of fun or experience a great deal of pleasure. But we must have one thing for happiness: we must have peace of mind, which is the opposite of mental conflict.

TORN BETWEEN TWO LOVERS

When we are finding it difficult to decide between two persons, two opportunities, or two things, we are experiencing what psychologists call mental conflict or cognitive dissonance. This "mental civil war" develops when the perceived advantages of one alternative counterbalance the perceived advantages of another alternative or when the disadvantages of one option seem to equal those of another.

The following are examples of indecision characterizing two different kinds of mental conflict.

First, **"approach-approach"** mental conflict, which is

portrayed in a song, "Torn between two lovers; Feeling like a fool; Loving both of you; Breaking all the rules." A *decision* must be made by the person described in this song if the "torn" feeling, the mental conflict, is to be overcome. A *choice* must be made if one is to enjoy peace of mind.

Second is **"avoidance-avoidance"** mental conflict, which is exemplified by the indecision of a woman who wants to avoid what she regards to be an undesirable outcome either way she chooses. She has a congenial but boring relationship with her husband. Most people would consider him to be a good man, but she wishes she were married to someone more exciting. Although she greedily launches into an affair, she decides to remain married because her husband is a capable father and is financially successful. Eventually he learns of her affair and gives her an ultimatum to decide to be true to him or to prepare for divorce. She does not want a divorce and does not want to give up her other man. She begins to experience "avoidance-avoidance" mental conflict. She wants to avoid losing her husband as well as her lover.

This woman can free herself from the agony of her mental conflict only after she *chooses* one man and gives up the other. Most of us are not willing to let go of our greed and choose one option instead of another until after we have suffered a degree of emotional anguish from being "torn between two lovers," torn between two career opportunities, and so on.

An attitude of greed is often the cause for one's mental conflict and indecision. Getting rid of greed, then, is the beginning of choosing; and once a choice is made—once a definite decision is made—then peace of mind will be regained and there no longer will be mental conflict.

Trivial Versus Crucial Decisions

Make decisions quickly when they pertain to trivial, unimportant matters, like choosing a certain flavor of gum or ice cream when in fact you like all flavors or trying to decide what color blouse or shirt to wear when all the colors that you have hanging in your closet will go very well with the jeans that you are wearing. Make slowly and carefully those decisions that are of crucial importance. A decision is crucial whenever its outcome can have far-reaching consequences, when its influence can continue for years and sometimes forever. Two of the most important decisions that most people ever make are whom to marry and what career to pursue.

Here are four steps in making important decisions:

First, *get all the information you can* on your topic of decision. When your decision is based on knowledge—on sound information—you are better able to choose wisely and act with a feeling of certainty. We can make an important decision with more calmness and confidence if we are careful to obtain important information on the issue. We can do this by reading; getting advice from professionals, family members, and friends; doing consumer research through the web; and so forth. Second, *carefully compare all the aspects of one alternative to those of another.* For instance, suppose you want to make a decision about a career and you've narrowed the alternatives to business, computer science, and education. To begin with, compare the advantages and disadvantages of a career in business to those of computer science, assigning each feature a value from zero to ten points. If you have given business a greater number of total points, then repeat the process by comparing the positives and negatives of business to those of a career in education.

Third, *make a choice*, a tentative decision, based on the greatest number of points. But don't feel compelled to act immediately on your choice. You probably will have time to wait a while before acting on your decision. The purpose of waiting is to see whether additional information that you might obtain will alter your thinking and to see if your feelings remain firm in favor of your tentative choice.

Fourth, *finalize your decision and act on it.* No decision is complete until one has acted upon it. Courage, which is deciding and acting in spite of fear, not without fear, is required whenever we make an important decision. If we had no fear, there would be no need for courage.

DARE TO DECIDE

Psychologist Bruno Bettelheim notes that although it is

commonly thought that people who have ego strength are decisive, it is even more true that people who dare to decide have ego strength. In other words, the act of deciding strengthens one's ego and builds self-confidence.

We tend to live as we talk. Therefore, speaking with words that denote decisions and commitment will strengthen our abilities to decide. In contrast, the sloppy habit of speaking with excessive hedge terms will weaken our decision-making abilities. We are hedging when we use terms like: "I don't know" when we really do know and terms like "Maybe" and "I'll try" instead of saying "I will."

Deciding with stability will enhance our success and happiness; deciding with instability will detract from our success and happiness. Stability means we stay with our choices and are not wishy-washy, vacillating back and forth. In other words, once you've carefully decided, don't get wiggly.

By choosing, we create ourselves, to a great extent. If I choose to be a professor and follow my decision with the necessary action, then I am a professor. If you choose to be an artist or a salesman and follow your decision with the necessary action, then you are what you have chosen to be.

The people who are the happiest are those who make a decision and then put the matter out of their minds instead of going over and over it and worrying about whether they made the right choice.

We often hear someone say, "I must make the right decision." But most of our decisions do not involve one "right" choice. This is true even when we are making a very important decision, such as the choice of a marriage partner or a career. Most of us could be happily married to any one of a large number of individuals, and most of us could be successful in any one of a number of different careers. Let's avoid the habit of getting hung up in a state of indecision because we erroneously think there is one "right" alternative. Instead, carefully decide in favor of one of your options, and then make your decision right by your follow-through action. By doing this, you free yourself from mental conflict.

17

Anxiety—Avoiding It and

Overcoming It

O NE OF THE most common negative emotions is anxiety. It is like fear, but it is different from fear. We feel fear when we believe our physical being is in danger. If our car goes out of control on an icy mountain pass, we may be gripped with fear. Anxiety, on the other hand, comes to us when we believe we are threatened in nonphysical ways. Fear of making the wrong decision, fear of what other people will think, fear of the future, and fear of failure are major causes of anxiety. Whatever we can do to avoid or overcome anxiety is important because anxiety can bring on insomnia, a dulling of the senses, and an inability to think clearly and act effectively.

Most of us experience anxiety when we are facing an important decision. The anxiety may lead us to put off the decision for fear of being wrong. This is normal because important decisions can have far-reaching consequences in our lives. However, procrastination will intensify our anxiety. Indecision brings even more anxiety than the experience of making an important decision. To go on undecided when we know that a decision has to be made brings both anxiety and feelings of guilt. This is true because we hold ourselves responsible for our indecision as well as our decision.

Uncertainty Causes Anxiety

Kierkegaard taught that anxiety is the in-between of the potential and the actual. By making a decision, we move from the potential to the actual, from the uncertain to the certain. Once we decide and act on our decision, the anxiety subsides.

Most of us experience anxiety, according to psychologist Rollo May, when we are considering "abandoning" something that has been meaningful to us. Some examples are: considering giving up one's nationality or a different citizenship; changing from one religion to another or abandoning religion entirely; changing one's place of residence; divorcing one's marriage partner. Such contemplations stir up anxiety because we can never be entirely certain about what a major change will bring into our lives. Just realizing that anxiety is normal at times like these can help reduce the apprehension we feel.

Concern about the reactions of others is a major cause of anxiety. It is important that we consider the wishes and needs of others, but we need to avoid overconcern about what other people might think about what we do and say. Most people are not judging us as harshly as we may believe. Worrying about what people will think brings anxiety and blocks our spontaneity. Because we cannot always win the approval of others, approval-seeking behavior guarantees anxiety.

Overconcern about how tomorrow or next year will turn out is an anxiety stimulus. Why is this so? Because all of us are uncertain about the future. Thus, if we focus our thoughts on the future, we are focusing on uncertainty, and this triggers anxiety. We can prevent and overcome "futuristic" anxiety by habitually tuning in to the present. The future will take care of itself. The present moment is the only time that any of us has. To reduce anxiety about the future, stop thinking about it. The New Testament tells us not to "worry about tomorrow; it will have enough worries of its own. There is no need to add to the troubles each day brings."[1]

Overconcern about success is another cause of anxiety. Psychologist Albert Ellis says an attitude of "I must" generates anxiety but an attitude of "I would like to" or "I would prefer to" is a sign of healthy concern. If a student tells herself, "I must get A grades on all my schoolwork," she will probably be anxious most of the time. Even though she now has a straight-A record, she is not free from anxiety because she knows it is possible that she might get a grade lower than an A, and she has indoctrinated herself to believe that she must always get an A. She can avoid a lot of anxiety by changing the terms "I must" to "I would prefer to" always get A grades. While concern improves our performance, anxiety weakens it.

In summary, we have the potential for anxiety when we are trying to make an important decision, when we are chronically undecided, when we are considering giving up something that has become significant, when we are overconcerned about the opinions and judgments of others, when we are overconcerned about the future, and when we fear that we will not accomplish what we have indoctrinated ourselves to believe that we *must* accomplish. Concern improves our performance, but anxiety undermines our performance and, consequently, our happiness.

NOTE

1. Matthew 6:34, Good News for Modern Man—The New Testament in Today's English Version.

Feeling Good—Taking Charge of Our Emotions

W E WILL HAVE better health and more happiness if we take charge of our emotions. What is an emotion? It is a feeling or mood that is felt throughout one's entire being.

Emotional states have their opposites: courage and fear, joy and sorrow, elation and depression, affection and anger, love and hate. Whenever we experience one of these emotions, a change occurs in the muscles, glands, and chemistry of the body.

Not only does an emotion bring about physiological changes in the body, but the reverse is also true. Biochemical and hormonal changes resulting from exercising, eating, sleeping, making love, or from taking some kind of medication, can change one's emotional state. Regular exercise, sufficient sleep, and good nutrition all engender positive emotions.

There are basically only four things that human beings can do: We can *emote*—that is, experience a certain emotion, feeling, or mood; we can *act*, which includes the performance of an activity such as writing, speaking, sleeping, dancing, making love, and so on; we can *think,* that is, form ideas and reach conclusions in our minds; finally, we can *have sense experiences* through our abilities to see, hear, taste, touch, and smell. To help you remember these four things, think of the key word **EATS.** This word stands for

Emote

Act

Think, and

Sense

You can change your *emotional state*—your mood, or your feelings—by changing your *actions*, your *thoughts,* and your *sense perceptions*. Acting, thinking, and sensing both trigger emotions and modify them. Emotions are like fire in the sense that they must have fuel to keep going. Our actions (which include our manner of speaking), the thoughts we choose, and the way we use our five senses all have the potential to act as fuel on fire, intensifying emotional states such as anger or depression.

ACTING TRIGGERS EMOTIONS

How can we change a negative emotion by changing our actions? It was the father of American psychology, William James, of Harvard, who taught that if you want to have a certain emotion, *act as if* you already feel that way. He said your action will help bring the feeling that you want. This became known as the William James "act as if" principle. Sometimes when I'm on my way to give a talk, I'm not in the mood to give it, but, after I begin speaking, I begin to get in the mood. My action of speaking helps bring about a change in my feeling.

Movie actors and actresses regularly use the "act as if" principle. If an actress is supposed to do a crying scene, she would probably not turn to the director and say, "I'm sorry, but I'm just not in the mood to cry today. I'll call you on the telephone when I feel like crying." And when an actor is supposed to do a "tough" scene, he would probably not say to the director, "I'm not in the mood. I don't feel like acting tough. I'll come around when I feel tough and you can have your camera crew come and shoot the scene." Instead, he clinches his fists. He walks tough and he talks tough, and his acting *as if* he feels tough soon brings the feeling to match the act. Of course, we would be phony if our actions were always different from our feelings. We only need to use the "act as if" principle temporarily, on those occasions when we want to change negative feelings into positive ones.

When the emotion of anger has erupted between a husband and wife, it is important that they *act as if* they still love each other as soon as possible. In this situation, two of the most effective actions that can be taken to change the feeling of anger to a feeling of love are speaking and touching. You can overcome much of your angry feeling toward your mate if you will make an effort to speak words of courtesy, kindness, and love, and if you will touch and embrace your partner. The sexual act can also be extremely effective in helping to restore feelings of love.

In her book, *The New Sex Therapy,* Helen Singer Kaplan tells how a loving sex experience can rejuvenate positive feelings in a marriage:

> Some patients report that the day after they have engaged in a particularly arousing sexual act with an especially loved and desired partner they experience profoundly pleasurable flashbacks. These are triggered by memories of the erotic experience and are accompanied by intense erotic sensations and feelings of euphoria and love. Heath has found that orgasm is associated with electrical discharges in the septal region of the brain. Stimulation of the septal region in humans is associated with intense feelings of love and affection and with reduction of anger and irritability.[1]

In a "loving marriage," sex is an act of love.

Remember, actions trigger emotions and change moods. Act the way you want to feel. This is taking charge of your emotions.

Thinking Triggers Emotions

Mark Twain had an experience that shows how one's thinking can influence his emotional state. He had spent two hours of a hot summer night trying to go to sleep at a friend's house. The bedroom had only one window, which was stuck. The stuffy atmosphere of the room was unbearable to a person accustomed to sleeping in fresh air from an open window. Finally in desperation in the darkness of the room, he threw his shoe at the window.

The crash of the glass signaled his mind to believe that fresh air was blowing in. The humorist inhaled deeply a few times and soon fell asleep. The next morning, to Mark Twain's astonishment, he discovered that his shoe had missed the window and had shattered the glass in the bookcase instead.

Even though the air in the bedroom remained stale throughout the night, Mark Twain was able to sleep well because of what he thought. His altered state of mind changed his mood or emotional state. This story magnifies the truth of Shakespeare's statement, "Nothing is either good or bad, but thinking makes it so." The point is, the way we *think* about positive and negative events determines to a great extent how we feel about them.

An attitude is *a way of thinking about a certain subject.* Thus, if one changes his attitude about something, it means he has changed his thinking about it, and a change in thinking triggers a change in feelings or emotions. To overcome negative feelings about something, then, one must learn to change his attitude or way of thinking about it.

How does worry relate to taking charge of one's emotions? *Worry is thought tinged with fear.* It's fretfully thinking about what has happened or might happen. Worry is thinking "in circles"— *rethinking* something over and over after it has already been thought through carefully. Like a rocking chair, worry keeps us busy, but doesn't get us anywhere.

To overcome worry, one must practice *CTC—Conscious Thought Control.* Taking charge of one's emotions means taking charge of one's mind. Even though one might be in miserable circumstances such as captivity, illness, or poverty, he is still free to choose his thoughts, and these thoughts will influence how he feels.

It is not the occurrence of a negative event that disturbs us emotionally, as much as it is our attitude toward the event. I thought myself into a state of emotional disturbance after I became partially blind. My irrational crooked thinking went like this: "I'm too young for blindness! It's unfair, it's unjust, it's unfortunate, and it's tragic."

Now many years later, I'm as blind as ever, but I am not as emotionally upset about my blindness. One of the main reasons for this is that I've changed my attitude. I have changed my crooked thinking into straight, realistic thinking. If we are to be happy, we must continually monitor our thoughts and our "silent sentence self-talk" because thinking triggers emotions. We can modify the proverb to say, "As a man thinketh, so shall his emotional state be."

SENSING TRIGGERS EMOTIONS

Sensing refers to our five senses: our ability to see, hear, taste, touch, and smell. You will remember that the letter S in our key word EATS stands for sense experience. If you're in a bad mood and you want to change it, try changing your sense experience. I've been in this room and in this building for hours, but in a few minutes, I'm going to go outside and walk. Feeling the fresh air, seeing the trees and sky, and hearing the birds, will give me an emotional lift. Also, many of us have used music and our sense of hearing to help us overcome our bad mood.

For more happiness, we must learn to lose our minds and find our senses. Psychiatrist Frederick Perls taught this concept to emphasize the fact that our senses have the power to rescue us from our thoughts. Constructive thinking is important but we must be cautious not to overanalyze, because this can paralyze our emotional health. Imagine the mental paralysis that might come to a centipede if, while lying on its back, it tries to decide which one of its many legs it should take off on after turning over.

The New Testament tells us that we cannot add to ourselves by worrying. We will enjoy life more if we worry less and sense more.

A sense of humor can be thought of as our sixth sense. If we're going to be happily married to ourselves, we must learn how to laugh. We are not born with a sense of humor; we have to develop it. Some people laugh, and others get mad, when they break a shoelace or run out of gas. It has been said that the measure of a man's maturity is the size of the things that make him mad. One time when I was cooking dinner, I grabbed what I thought was the large salt dispenser, but instead of salt, I had sprinkled cleanser on the carrots. Thanks to a sense of humor in our family, we had a pleasant meal anyway.

Whenever you begin to feel anger or anxiety or some other unpleasant emotion, remember you have the power to take charge of your emotions. Think of the key word EATS and give yourself immediate mental and physical first aid. Divert your mind to something else by turning on the TV or by listening to music or reading. Try various physical activities such as exercising, eating, and relaxing. Listening to a relaxation tape can be helpful. Physical as well as mental activities can help us overcome undesirable emotions because an emotion is experienced throughout the entire body. Remember, we can decrease the intensity of an unpleasant emotional state by changing how we act and how we think and how we use our five senses regarding an undesirable situation.

In conclusion, success, adjustment, and happiness are never permanently achieved by any of us, but must be continually worked at if they are to be experienced. The preamble to the United States Constitution guarantees life, liberty, and the pursuit of happiness. Notice that it does not guarantee happiness, only the pursuit of it; we must catch up to happiness ourselves.

NOTE

1. Helen Singer Kaplan, MD, PhD, *The New Sex Therapy* (New York: Brunner/Mazel, 1974), 14.

PART IV

Love in Your Marriage Can Be Forever

Could you have a happy marriage even if you did not have the freedom to choose your own partner? Yes, you could in most cases, provided you and your partner give your relationship what every good marriage needs. If you abuse and neglect your marriage, it will deteriorate. But if there is a mutual effort in your marriage to apply the information in this book, you will probably both enjoy a growing relationship.

Even though all love relationships are unique, there are certain characteristics in every good marriage. A successful marriage is a satisfying achievement which most couples can accomplish, if they put forth the effort to try marriage before divorce.

Divorcing and remarrying does not end one's marriage problems, but only gives them variation. This is why tuning-up is usually better than breaking up.

19

The Nuts and Bolts in Your

Love Machine

What Every Good Marriage Needs

IT IS NOW well over a quarter of a century since Eleanor and I made a commitment to each other. Our marriage has been successful because our relationship has been pleasant more often than unpleasant, and we have both contributed to the health, happiness, and progress of the other.

COMMITMENT

The fact that we are still together does not mean that we have not had "wrinkles" in our relationship and unpleasant times together. We have shared some very difficult experiences that have burdened our marriage. All couples have thorns in the roses of their relationships. People who remain married do so *not* because they've never had a reason to divorce, but because they have made a personal commitment to stay together even when trouble comes.

If there is an attitude of marrying tentatively "to see how it works out," it probably will not work out.

If you're considering marrying someone but don't want to make a commitment because you feel uncertain about this person, don't go through with the wedding. If you marry someone you have strong doubts about, you will find it very difficult to commit yourself for better or worse. Persons who maintain marital loyalty only when the partner is healthy, employed, and pleasant are not totally committed. Commitment means you've made a decision to be loyal to your partner in spite of negative experiences. A lack of commitment is one of the main causes for divorce. Every good marriage needs a man and woman who have the courage to commit themselves wholeheartedly to the relationship. Commitment means the couple will work to repair and maintain happiness in marriage.

TIME AND CARE

A couple who gives their relationship high priority among their overall activities takes time for each other and uses care in their manner of relating. If you want a good marriage, you've got to make yourself available to your partner often. While you're together, you both need to be aware of the kind of impression you're making on each other. Why should you try to make a good impression? Because marriage is the most important relationship you'll ever have. This is because it has the greatest potential to bring you either misery or joy. How can you make your time together a positive experience?

Merely being together in the same house is not enough. You also need to be mentally and emotionally tuned in to each other. A habit of spontaneously expressing positive feelings will make your time together more enjoyable and will strengthen your relationship. Whenever you have a positive thought or an affectionate feeling, express it in words and body language. Remember that the "act as if" principle in psychology is that feelings expressed are intensified. Feelings that are neither expressed by words or deeds gradually fade away and die.

This does not mean that all talk should be spontaneous. As my chapter on communication in this book implies, complaints and problems should be dealt with by appointment only. Hasty complaints and compulsive talk about problems detract from the enjoyment of one another's company. Refraining from expressing negative thoughts, while freely expressing positive ones helps a couple to enjoy their marriage.

HOW YOU ANSWER

In Proverbs we read, "A kind answer turns away wrath." Most of us have difficulty answering with kindness when someone is talking to us in an angry tone of voice, but I've learned that when I make an effort to answer anger with kindness, the other person usually moderates his or her voice. It's almost as if a tone of voice is contagious.

Your facial expression and overall body language can also elicit either a positive or negative response from your marriage partner. If your partner often responds to you negatively, it might be because of your body language more than because of what you are saying.

TOUCHING

Every good marriage needs touching and being touched. The message "I love you" can be powerfully communicated through appropriate touching. When a husband and wife stop talking and touching, their feelings of love will diminish. Both marriage partners must make a decision to often do gentle touching which is an expression of love. Holding hands, caressing, back scratching, massaging, hugging, cuddling, and so on are important to help satisfy touch hunger that we all have.

You're fortunate if you both desire about the same amount of affection.

Having grown up in a different family, your tendency to touch might be more or less than that of your mate. When this is true, the one who is less prone to touch needs to make a conscious effort to touch more often. All of us can change if we decide we want to. All self-induced change in human behavior begins with a decision. When there is a difference between a husband and wife in their propensity to touch, why should the change be in favor of more touching rather than less? It is because in a loving relationship, touch is usually an expression of love. Therefore, it is not something that one partner should leave entirely up to the other. Yet in a considerable number of marriages, one mate leaves this expression of love mainly up to the other.

Based on my counseling experience with hundreds of couples, I've concluded that wives are more remiss than husbands in touching. Some wives have explained that they are reluctant to touch because the husband seems to think that all touch has to lead to sex. Although some marriages would be improved if touching more often did result in sex, certain husbands need to learn to enjoy caressing even when it might not evolve into sexual lovemaking.

Somehow, in growing up, a considerable number of girls get the erroneous idea that expressing love physically, which includes touching, is entirely the responsibility of the guy. This is disappointing to men because they, as well as women, want to believe they are desirable enough to be sought after.

A wife who lovingly touches her husband, through her own initiative, will not only improve her own marriage but will also help her daughters prepare for a successful marriage. Parents are marriage-role models for their children, whether they realize it or not.

What about Sex?

Every good marriage needs a mutually satisfying sexual relationship.

Granted, it is more important to some individuals and couples than others, but I've seldom seen a marriage that had vitality unless there was sexual harmony.

In early marriage, husbands generally want sex more often than wives, but there is an increasing percentage of wives whose desire exceeds that of their husbands. A man told me that his wife would take him to the bedroom three times a day if she could. Some men might envy this husband, but most couples would not have the time to make love this often, even if they had the desire. Some wives, and many husbands, complain to me that their partner seldom, or never, initiates sexual lovemaking. A few husbands who've been married for as long as twenty years have told me that they cannot remember a single time when their wife initiated lovemaking. Because sex is an expression of love, isn't it reasonable that wives, as well as husbands, should initiate it?

One man told me that for over ten years his wife had never

completely undressed for lovemaking except when he insisted, and she has never intentionally allowed him to see her undressed. One who neglects physical love, ranging from touch to sex, must recognize this as a deficiency in the art of loving and resolve to overcome it.

Fair Play concerning Work

Every good marriage needs partners who have a sense of fairness. In certain other marriages, husbands are more fair than wives. An increasing number of husbands are describing to me situations in their homes that could be interpreted as unfair behavior on the part of the wife. A number of husbands have said they have to prepare their own breakfast even though the wife is not employed. One man has a daily routine of cooking his own breakfast, putting up his own lunch, and working at hard manual labor all day. Some of these husbands say they don't mind having to prepare their own breakfast as much as having to eat it alone. Family members who are going off to school and work deserve the company and farewell of those who are remaining at home.

One businessman said he does most of the housecleaning even though his wife is unemployed. He explained that if he doesn't do it, it doesn't get done.

Homemaking can be an interesting occupation. If more husbands would compliment their wives concerning their homemaking accomplishments, more women would find homemaking rewarding and enjoyable. Have you ever heard anyone say in essence, "I am the way I am and I'm not going to change for anyone"? A person who has this attitude is not ready for marriage or any close relationship. As you've read in the chapter "Adjustment in Marriage Means Change—The 5 C's," any good marriage is characterized by ongoing changes. For a happy marriage, you don't have to change your basic personality, but you must be willing to change certain aspects of your manner of relating to your mate. To repent means to change, and every good marriage needs both a husband and a wife who are willing to do ongoing repenting. A man or woman who is unwilling to make changes for the mutual enjoyment and success of the relationship should remain single.

Forgiving is just as important as repenting for happiness in human relations. Forgiving is so important for mental and physical health as well as for marriage happiness that it needs to be emphasized. We must forgive despite the continuing imperfections of the other person. It impairs our health and happiness when we refuse to forgive someone whom we think has not yet earned our forgiveness. We place a heavy burden on ourselves to have judged someone, to have found him guilty, and to have decided to punish him by retaining resentment and anger. The New Testament counsels, "Let all bitterness, and wrath, and anger, and clamour, and evil speaking, be put away from you, with all malice: And be kind one to another, tenderhearted, forgiving one another."[1]

A man told me that he had been holding a grudge against one of his family members for four years and had just discovered that the recipient of his resentment didn't even know about it. Obviously, this man's refusal to forgive had harmed nobody but himself.

I advised a wife to forgive her husband who had been unfaithful to her.

She tried to assure me that she had forgiven him, but added that since he had committed adultery she could hardly stand to look at him. I told her that had she truly forgiven her husband she would not find his company so repulsive. She had forgiven in theory but not in practice. Merely saying that one has forgiven somebody does not necessarily mean that there has been true forgiveness. I asked this woman to seriously consider the statement that once a deep injury is done us we never recover until we forgive. The most important reason we should forgive a spouse, or anyone who has wronged us, is for our own health and happiness. Because adultery can be very damaging to the happiness of a marriage and family, no one could be more opposed to it than I, yet it usually does not necessitate divorce. Sexual transgression sometimes precipitates a divorce, either because one spouse persists in it, or because the other refuses to forgive.

When a couple is in this kind of crisis, it is of crucial importance that they get the right kind of professional help if they are to save their marriage. Helping a couple reconcile after infidelity is very satisfying for me as well as for them. Even when a marriage is in shambles, it is not doomed to destruction if both are willing to repent and forgive.

IS YOUR MARRIAGE A MUTUAL IMPROVEMENT ASSOCIATION?

The close relationship of marriage is an opportunity for ongoing personal growth if you are both willing to give and receive constructive feedback. Think of the ways in which you are a better person because of what you've learned from your partner. When I've known someone who repeatedly blunders by saying something that's inaccurate, or by doing something that would be offensive to others, I've wondered, "Why doesn't this individual's marriage partner correct him or her on this?"

If you want to be a grower, regularly ask your husband or wife for an opinion on what you are doing or saying or wearing. My wife has studied and taught the subject of clothing through family and consumer sciences; therefore, I often ask her opinion on what to wear with what, and I usually have her accompany me when I shop for clothing.

You can also widen your world through marriage, as well as improve yourself. Through your marriage partner you can expand your social circle. Before I met Eleanor I don't think she had ever watched a horse race. I'm now fond of avocados and she watches the Kentucky Derby with me on television every spring.

Every good marriage needs a husband and wife who accentuate the positives rather than the negatives, who make the most of what they have and the least of what they do not have.

WOULD YOU QUALIFY FOR A MARRIAGE PROMOTION?

If you and your mate have an agreement that at the end of the year each of you could be rewarded with a marriage promotion, do you think you would qualify? In our occupations most of us work diligently for merit pay and promotions. Every good marriage needs a husband and wife who take their marriage as seriously as they do their careers. In our employment, if we have a ho-hum attitude and show a lack of effort, we will not be promoted, and might even be fired. In a satisfying marriage, each partner makes an ongoing effort to perform well as a husband or wife. Most mediocre marriages are characterized by neglect rather than abuse.

Many breakfast cereals are enriched with minerals and vitamins. Persons who deserve a marriage promotion do things often to enrich their relationship and make it more enjoyable. We don't always need to work at our marriage, but we do need to form the habit of consistently expressing love, giving compliments, and doing favors for each other. If you do this, your partner will love you more for it and you will like yourself better. Plan to have a good talk every day and dress up and go out together at least once a week. You don't have to spend money every time. For some of your dates, you can do things such as visit friends, attend free concerts, and go to church.

If you really believe your partner would give you a marriage promotion, you are to be commended. Remember, a quality relationship is not an accident. It is an achievement.

Qualities of a Good Marriage

Here is a review of the qualities that every good marriage needs:

1. A whole-hearted commitment to the marriage from both the husband and the wife.
2. To be pleasant more often than unpleasant. A relationship in which each partner contributes to the health, happiness, progress, and success of the other.
3. Priority time together for communication, affection, and recreation.
4. Speaking and acting with kindness more often than with unkindness.
5. Touching and the initiation of lovemaking by the wife as well as the husband.
6. Fair play concerning work.
7. Partners who will repeatedly repent of their marital offenses and forgive one another.
8. A husband and wife who will help each other improve and expand personal horizons.

9. A couple who accentuates the positives in marriage and everyday life.

10. A husband and wife who would individually qualify for a "marriage promotion."

NOTE

1. Ephesians 4:31–32.

20

Comments from Those in the Driver's Seat

THE FOLLOWING STATEMENTS were written by some husbands and wives with whom I am acquainted. I asked them to comment on what they believe every good marriage needs.

※

We have been married over forty years. I believe it isn't any one particular thing, but rather a combination of many things that has made our marriage successful. Although it is probably true that anyone of a number of things could wreck a marriage, seldom does only one thing make a marriage successful.

What is it that has kept us happily married for over forty years? We agree that it is mutual respect, complete trust, and an open line of communication. But most of the credit has to go to Lois Ann. When I arrive home in the evenings, she always has her hair fixed nicely, and has a clean dress on and a smile to greet me. She truly makes the house a haven of rest and relaxation. The old saying that "The way to a man's heart is through his stomach" has been true in our home. All this was true of her, even when our children were small.

We agree that we are more in love now than when we were younger, and it is harder to be separated than it used to be.

The most important thing in our marriage, the one above all others that has kept us together and happy, is our love for each other, including physical love. My wife has always been a responsive love partner. A satisfying sex life is probably the real mortar that holds the bricks together of what has been a very satisfying forty years, and keeps things from tilting out of balance. Periods of separation or other unpleasantness can be endured because we both know full well how much fun is waiting at the end of the separation, and there is no one either of us would rather be with. We look forward to many more enjoyable years together in this life and don't see how heaven could possibly be the wonderful place it is reported to be, without each other in a continuing family relationship.

Elmer Foutz

❧

The embryo . . . the seed . . . the very life line that sparks the whole episode of a dynamic love relationship Yes, the electricity that starts and keeps that energy flowing is the magic of "Romance." Some might think that I'm a romantic, and I gladly confess that I am, because I am convinced that if we are to have a joyous marriage, this quality must stay with us. Romance is not just a happenstance, but it comes into being because we care for someone else enough to keep it alive.

It's important that we pause frequently and ask ourselves if we still get a thrill when we see the face or hear the voice of our companion. Do we still want to look our best, act our best, be as courteous, as attentive as we were before marriage? If we take each other for granted, I can only believe our life together will be little more than hum-drum.

The energy involved in romance is positive! If we make the effort to capture and nourish it, I know it can he maintained forever, and will keep our marriage young and alive. Therefore romance, to me, is one of the most vital and important elements of a successful marriage.

Charles Beyers, married 35 years

❧

If a marriage is to endure with mutual satisfaction, the man and woman must enjoy each other's company and conversation a majority of the time. As demands of family and career increase, a husband and wife may find it more and more difficult to find time to enjoy each other, and to communicate effectively. A couple needs to arrange for daily and weekly times to be together alone, to discuss the little things as well as matters of importance. A daily walk together can provide a private, invigorating setting for good conversation. The combined physical and emotional benefits of such a daily habit could reduce the tensions that tend to build in a marriage. A weekly date together for dinner, a movie, or another mutually enjoyable activity can also have a therapeutic value that far exceeds the costs involved.

Larry Tippetts

❧

One of the most important things that we think a good marriage needs is the ability to recognize that there's a problem and to be willing to work it out. Couples need to *recognize* when the problem is bigger than themselves, and to search out someone with whom to consult, preferably with a religious background. We have spiritual needs as well as physical and emotional needs.

We believe that one thing that has probably contributed most to making our marriage happy is our ability to try to make it better every day. We are just like a garden, our little problems have to be weeded out on a daily basis. Just as a garden needs to be cultivated, fertilized, and watered for proper growth, a marriage also needs to be carefully tended with little "I love you," "I'm sorry," love pats, etc.

Dick and Dilla Hunter

❦

I think one of the key ingredients to a successful and lasting marriage relationship is a mutual trust and confidence. This is established early in the courtship experience and must be reinforced and solidified by positive experience early in the marriage.

Many people have little problem developing and enjoying a trustworthy relationship. While for others, basic personality traits coupled with the environmental condition in which they were raised tend to result in their being more insecure and uncertain of those whom they can trust.

Distrust in a relationship as intimate as marriage soon grows and affects many of the other areas of the relationship, and has the effect of polarizing the marriage partners instead of bonding them closer to each other.

Paul H. Foster

❦

Beginning with the basic premise that the marriage began with compatible partners who mated for love, I think the most important quality for continuing success in marriage is affection. By this, I mean the couple communicates on a daily basis by a touch, a smile, a look, and a compliment.

Other ways to show affection could be doing an unexpected chore, keeping the children busy to allow the partner a quiet time alone, fixing a favorite meal, or bringing home a pizza after a busy day. If one searches a bit, new ways of showing affection can be found almost daily to keep the spice in the marriage.

Barbara Smith, married eight years

❧

An important key that is necessary for happiness in marriage is maturity.

I believe that maturity is best characterized as unselfishness. Next (in order of importance) I believe to be prayer. Many a marriage has been transformed by initiating practice of regular prayer.

William "B" Pethtel, married seventeen years

❧

What every couple needs is time alone. Not just those daily and weekly moments over coffee, a walk, or an evening out for dinner. As important as these are, they are not enough. What I am referring to is time away from the home front for two or three days, several times a year where, no longer parents and home managers, the couple can be sweethearts once again.

These short trips each year have played a large part in keeping romance alive and well in our marriage for its duration of fifteen years. Our trysting place is about a hundred miles from home—a favorite room in a mountain inn where three or four times a year we escape our daily roles. During those forty-eight to seventy-two-hour stays, we eat out, sleep in, browse through shops, play chess, and take walks with camera in hand. Gary and I make it a point to keep talk of the children to a minimum, for this time is ours to share hopes, dreams, and sometimes our fears.

You may be thinking, "We can't afford it." But if *we* can, *you* can. Gary works for wages and makes less than $40,000 a year; yet these trips are planned into the budget just like insurance premiums, power bills, and family vacation.

Our three sons think our short trips are a normal part of life. They've never complained about being left home. An additional benefit has been the unity they see in us. They know our love is strong and we never have any trouble with them trying to play one of us against the other. Someone once said, "The greatest gift a father can give his children is that of loving their mother." I think he is right.

Joy LePage Smith

❧

I think in order to have a successful marriage there has to be a certain kind of loyalty, which encompasses the emotional side, as well as the physical side of marriage.

Distrust comes into the marriage, when instead of talking the problem over with your mate, you take it to a friend or family member—you've got it talked over and you feel better, but you haven't talked it over with your partner.

Your first loyalty in marriage should be to communicate your good feelings along with the hurt. The second part of being loyal deals with cooperatively accomplishing physical tasks such as maintenance of a yard, a home, a car, and caring for the children. This physical loyalty also includes the maintenance of the love relationship and the desire to give individual time to each other.

Geri Hazen

❧

I think an important quality in marriage is expressing appreciation to have the ability to understand, to admire, to enjoy, and to cherish.

It is usually easy for us to see the faults and weaknesses of our spouse, but hard for us to recognize these same weaknesses in ourselves. It is easy for us to make, what seems to us, logical and sound excuses for our shortcomings, but hard for us to forgive the faults of others.

Instead of faultfinding, we need to stop at the end of each day and thank God for our marriage. It is very easy, as the years pass by, to take one another for granted, and to begin thinking, "What is this marriage really doing for me?" Instead, we must realize that the main source of happiness is within ourselves. It *is* unreasonable for us to expect our husband or wife to make us happy and to solve our problems. A husband and wife are more likely to have a good marriage it they try to recognize each other's qualities and express appreciation for them.

Sherryl Dunn Whittaker

❧

Every good marriage needs trust. A partner with self-esteem is more likely to believe in the honesty, integrity, and reliability of the other, and this positive attitude is usually reciprocated.

Trusting partners can accept the need a spouse may have to be alone sometimes and will not be jealous if a husband or wife participates in an activity which does not include both partners.

In a trusting relationship, when a spouse says, "I'm sorry, I was wrong," the apology is accepted and the disagreement settled. When you trust your partner you don't hold grudges because you know the apology is genuine, and you believe that person will speak the truth.

When your marriage is built on trust you will be able to rely on each other. If a partner says an effort will be made to change an attitude or accomplish a task, you will know that he or she will do everything possible to achieve this goal. You trust it will be done.

Jill Cooper

❧

One of the most important elements of a successful marriage is a mutual give-and-take relationship. Marriage partners cannot both expect to do exactly as they want without regard for their mate. An unequal relationship will create resentment from the "loser." The workable balance for any particular marriage depends on the couple involved, their circumstances and the use of common sense. Necessarily, each person must give up some freedoms for the other, but the benefits gained in return are worth it.

Shelley Servatius

۶

Every good marriage needs a "friendly atmosphere." Somewhere between marriage and six children, I have come to realize that my wife is indeed my best friend, and that we were first in love, and later best friends. Some may say that all this is backwards, and that friendship should come before love and marriage. But the need to communicate with your mate about finances, sibling rivalries, and neighborhood squabbles becomes more valuable and needed as a marriage progresses.

Children eventually leave the family nest, and husband and wife had better be friends when that happens, because they still have lots of marriage time left after the children are gone. Many late-night friendly talks can make a marriage "alive and well," and as I consider the friends that I have had during my life, my wife is by far my best friend.

Phil Boren

۶

A successful marriage is a well-woven blend of many different elements, one of the most important being open and honest communication between both partners. When the communication lines are open between both the senders and receivers, feelings of neglect and unfairness are reduced.

Rex Wheeler

۶

What every couple needs most is a deep abiding belief that God has a plan for their lives—that their "couple love" can make a difference in a chaotic world. Such a belief will carry them through days when they feel like giving up.

Children of such a marriage are seen as gifts from God, yet the couple is acutely aware of the responsibility that comes with the package—not only to love the children and meet their needs, but to discipline and teach them as well. In this setting, as is true with their children, the couple finds their individual characters are deepened and enriched while they work, love, pray, and play together.

Without this belief, it is easy for a couple to become confused and wonder what purpose there is in the hard work and sacrifice marriage and family life bring. Loving one another is not enough. But a couple that shares the belief that they are a working vital part of the Divine Plan can find maximum fulfillment in marriage.

Joy LePage Smith

21

Tuning Up Your Marriage Is Usually Better Than Breaking Up

Do You Need a Divorce?

Should you divorce if your romantic love has dwindled to smoldering coals? No, not necessarily. This alone is insufficient reason to divorce, because feelings of love can be rekindled. A feeling of love is an emotional state, which can be changed by anybody who has learned how to take charge of his or her emotions. I refer you to the scientific research later in this chapter about unhappily married couples who remain in the marriage and five years later report happy marriages.

Don't Burn Down Your House

If your relationship is like most marriages, it just needs a tune-up. You, as a couple, might rejuvenate your marriage by reading good marriage books or by talking with someone you trust, such as your clergyman, or by participating in a couples growth group or a marriage enrichment weekend retreat.

You do not necessarily need a divorce even if you think your relationship needs a major overhaul. You would not junk an expensive car just because of a need for repairs. Neither would you burn down your house to get rid of mice. You have a much greater investment in your marriage, and it is far more precious to you. Therefore, even if you believe your marriage is in serious trouble, resort to courtship—not to court—and get help from a competent marriage and family counselor who is *pro-marriage* and believes that most marriages are worth saving.

If you believe your marriage has potential for success, but you as a couple do not find the help you need from the first counselor with whom you consult, confer with several other marriage therapists until you find one who can give you the help that you need in order to build a successful marriage. Tuning up your marriage is usually much better than breaking up.

Some couples marry impulsively without having been careful to choose someone whose values, lifestyles, and life goals are the same as theirs. They may not have the potential for a lifetime of happiness together.

Emotional Trauma from Divorce

Compared to all other negative events in one's life, divorce probably has the greatest potential for emotional trauma except for the unexpected death of a loved one.

A mother of four young children told me of her disenchantment with her professor husband. She quickly decided to divorce. I tried to persuade her to reconsider because I knew her husband was a good man in an honorable profession. They could build a successful marriage, I thought, with some guidance. But she was not receptive to this recommendation and promptly went through with her divorce plans. Divorce for her was traumatic. There was not enough money. She was lonely. The other man she had hoped to marry decided against her. She had no relatives nearby for psychological support. Her physical health deteriorated, and she plummeted emotionally. While her marriage had been disappointing, her single life was now depressing.

On the other hand, divorce is the best solution for some spouses in unrewarding relationships, but not for most. Divorce can bring relief or regret, gain or loss, hope or despair, health or illness. The term for better or worse applies to divorce as well as marriage.

The vast majority of relationship problems are solvable and the vast majority of marriages are worth the effort required to make them work.

People in the throes of marital problems who are considering divorce, need to get the message that working it out instead of getting out is a viable solution.[1]

CAN YOU FULLY DIVORCE?

Even though there is disappointment and conflict in a marriage, a couple may still have a strong emotional bond. When this is true, divorce has high potential for trauma. Ending such a marriage is more like tearing fabric than paper.

Some mental health professionals believe that couples who have had a long, close relationship cannot fully divorce in the emotional sense. Legally they can end their marriage, but there are memories and emotional overtones that will always remain. Once meat and vegetables have been cooked into a stew, it is impossible to completely separate all the different ingredients again. This is also true for many couples who try to end their relationships.

Bereavement and grief are emotional states that can result from divorce as well as death. This is most often true for the spouse who did not want the divorce. After being divorced against his or her will, one might also lose custody of the children. According to the director of a suicide prevention center, men are more likely than women to commit suicide following divorce. This is probably because divorced men, more often than women, move out of the family home and lose custody of their children. How is adjustment accomplished? One needs to realize that adjusting to divorce might take a long time.

This is because divorce is more a process than an event. It is courtship in reverse. Individuals who've decided to divorce usually allow their marriage to gradually die before they end it legally. But even after a divorce decree, the relationship often continues for a long time, especially when there are young children.

The partner who loses the most from the divorce can be expected to suffer the greatest mental depression. In making the adjustment, one may need to do "grief work" as if a loved one had unexpectedly died. This includes allowing oneself to feel bad and to express these feelings appropriately. For a complete adjustment, one must permit the married self of yesterday to die and the divorced self of today to be born. This acceptance of reality is necessary if emotional equilibrium is to be regained.

A qualified marriage counselor or psychotherapist can teach divorced persons how to avoid wallowing in their emotional mire and guide them to recovery.

REGRETS ABOUT DIVORCE

A majority of divorced men and women, in a Wisconsin and Virginia study conducted by Dr. Mavis Hetherington, said that instead of obtaining a divorce they felt they should have worked harder at making their marriage a success. One year after their divorce, 60 percent of the men and 73 percent of the women concluded their choice to divorce was a mistake. Trauma was experienced by many.

According to this study, after divorce, the kinds of problems you can expect are daily routines being upset, emotional stress, economic hardship, disappointing social life, lack of sexual fulfillment, and parent/child difficulties.[2]

Diane Medved, nationally known author, decided to write a book about divorce. It was her intention to take a morally neutral position, but after many interviews and extensive research, she

> discovered the . . . aftermath of divorce is so pervasively disastrous—to body, mind and spirit—that in an overwhelming number of cases the "cure" that it brings is surely worse than the marriage's "disease."
>
> When I look at the balance of the bad and the good that divorced individuals endure, my only possible conclusion is that people could be spared enormous suffering if they scotched their permissive acceptance of divorce and viewed marriage as a serious, lifelong commitment, a bond not to be entered into—or wriggled out of—lightly.[3]

After divorce, men and women experience upsets in their daily routines, and both report insomnia. For the children, bedtime is more erratic, reading to them tends to be neglected, and family members eat together less often.

The researchers also reported that, after divorce, many men and women suffer severe emotional stress such as loneliness, anxiety, depression, anger, and a loss of self-confidence and self-esteem. Men, especially, feel uprooted, and both sexes feel unloved and unwanted. Emotionally induced illnesses are common, and sometimes serious ailments develop and remain. Performance at work can deteriorate so much that one's job is in jeopardy.

There is greater economic stress among divorced couples than among married couples. Children are involved in most divorces, and parents have the financial burden of supporting two households. Many ex-wives must take employment and be homemakers and mothers as well. To supplement their income, divorced parents often feel compelled to work at two or three jobs.

Most social activities in our society are couple oriented. While both sexes may feel shut out from many social events, single women with young children, and a low income, especially might feel trapped at home. Although having the freedom to date might be exciting for some persons who are newly divorced, most people soon have a need to settle down in a trusting relationship.

One of the most important factors in improving one's self-concept and regaining self-esteem after divorce is to succeed at reestablishing one's self in a loving relationship.

"When people divorce they have visions of better lives. Old problems will vanish, they hope, as new dreams take their place. These dreams usually include meeting candidates for more intimate status, and more freedom to pursue personal goals. These dreams frequently do not materialize, creating a new set of problems."[4]

WEEKEND FATHERS

Divorcing parents face additional problems. Fathers are more often deprived of their children's companionship because mothers usually gain custody. Most men at best are relegated to the role of a weekend "fun and games" father, and some fade out of their children's lives entirely because of high mobility. Great distances between ex-spouses help explain the fact that thousands of children are kidnapped every year by their own parents.

Concerning their feeling of loss, several fathers reported that "they could not endure the pain of seeing their children only intermittently and by two years after divorce had coped with this stress by seeing their children infrequently although they continued to experience a great sense of loss and depression."[5]

No matter how she might try, a mother cannot fully take the place of a father. This is especially true of a single woman with sons. "The mother-son relationship is particularly problematic in divorced families."

Children of Divorce

Every year millions of children suffer a form of bereavement because of their parents' divorce and their being deprived of the daily companionship of one of those parents. In most cases, children have feelings of love for both parents. Emotional trauma among the children in a family is most pronounced when their parents' separation and subsequent divorce comes unexpectedly and takes them by surprise. For the child who thinks his parents love each other, the news that they are going to divorce comes as a shock. On the other hand, if divorcing parents have chronically displayed hostility before their children, then the announcement of their plan to divorce might come as a relief to these children.

Virtually every child hopes his parents will work things out and remain married. For example, a young husband and wife were arguing and began contemplating divorce. Their ten-year-old boy persuaded them not to divorce. They are still together and have been married for over fifty years.

Bob, reflecting six years after his marriage broke up: "[The situation is] very sad. If I were a man of words I could tell you. But seeing the kids and leaving—it breaks my heart."

"Bob longs for his children but feels usurped by [his ex-wife's] second husband. He says, 'my children don't need me anymore.' With his fragile identity as father and husband, Bob is vulnerable to displacement by the person who is, in his view, the 'real man.' Intimidated by the psychological stresses attached to visiting his children, he is also overcome by financial burdens in the post divorce period.

He feels unimportant, not needed, and unloved . . ."

"Most young fathers in our study—those in their mid to late thirties at the ten-year mark—have not had sole or shared custody of their children at any point in the ten years, nor have they wished to have it. Instead, they visit with their children and their images of themselves as fathers are seriously impaired" "Being a father in a divorced or remarried family is a lot harder than being a father in an intact family."[6]

"Most fathers in this study fall in between. They tend to maintain frequent contact with their children but gradually visit less as the difficulties of maintaining a relationship loom larger as they are caught up in second marriages with new children and stepchildren as well as new jobs, new communities, new concerns."[7]

What impact can divorce have on the mental health and happiness of children?

> The mainstream media, liberal politicians, activists, and academia bewail child poverty in the U.S. But in these ritual lamentations, one key fact remains hidden: The principal cause of child poverty in the U.S. is the absence of married fathers in the home.
>
> According to the U.S. Census, the poverty rate in 2008 for single parents with children was 35.6 percent. The rate for married couples with children was 6.4 percent. Being raised in a married family reduces a child's probability of living in poverty by about 80 percent.
>
> . . . The positive effects of married fathers are not limited to income alone. Children raised by married parents have substantially better life outcomes compared to similar children raised in single-parent homes. When compared to children in intact married homes, children raised by single parents are more likely to have emotional and behavioral problems; be physically abused; smoke, drink, and use drugs; be aggressive; engage in violent, delinquent, and criminal behavior; have poor school performance; be expelled from school; and drop out of high school.[8]

SCIENTIFIC TRUTHS ABOUT MARRIAGE AND DIVORCE

Maggie Gallagher, an American author and commentator, has written about why we need marriage, comparing married people to those who are single. She cited scientific research that revealed married people are happier, healthier, and wealthier and have children who do better. People who have chosen to marry and who have been careful to create and re-create a happy marriage are better off in virtually every way than those who are single.[9]

> Linda Waite, a top family scholar at the University of Chicago, and Maggie Gallagher, Director of the Marriage Program at the Institute for American Values, have put together the case for [marriage] as you've never heard it before. A decade of research has yielded solid, scientific evidence: [that] marriage has powerful positive, transformative effects on both the adults who 'do it' and their children.
>
> Health, happiness, earnings, wealth, long life, better kids, great sex—in just about every dimension life science can measure, you are better off married than single.[10]

Findings based on national survey data that extensively measured personal and marital happiness revealed that:

> With the important exception of helping spouses escape violent marriages, divorce typically failed to deliver the promised psychological benefits for adults. Five years later, unhappily married adults who divorced or separated were, on average, no happier, no less depressed, had no higher self-esteem, no greater sense of personal mastery, and showed increased alcohol use compared to unhappily married adults who stayed married. Almost two thirds of unhappy spouses who stuck with the marriage forged happy marriages down the road . . . Does divorce typically make unhappily married people happier than staying married? No. Does a firm commitment to staying married, even though unhappy, typically condemn adults to lifelong misery? No.
>
> Is divorce always wrong and staying married always right? We cannot draw so simplistic a conclusion. What we do know is this: Both divorce and marriages initiate complex chains of events whose outcomes cannot be predicted with certainty at the outset. Marriages are not happy or unhappy—spouses are. And with the passage of time, the feelings of spouses about their marriages can and do change.[11]

"In most cases, a strong commitment to staying married not only helps couples avoid divorce, it helps more couples achieve a happier marriage."[12]

CIRCUMSTANCES THAT MIGHT JUSTIFY DIVORCE

In the beginning you might have been fully satisfied with the qualities of your marriage partner and with the blend of your relationship, but now there's trouble. Your partner's behavior is not only self-defeating but could ultimately be self-destructive. Chronic unemployment, conviction of a crime, gambling, or use of drugs, including alcohol, can undermine the health and happiness of both husband and wife.

After ten years of marital disappointment, a thirty-year-old woman sought my guidance. She was wondering about divorce, but before considering this option with her further, I wanted to hear her husband's side of the story. He was invited to join us in counseling, which he did for two sessions. But she was not convinced that he would make enough changes to satisfy her, and so she decided to divorce.

Soon after ending her marriage, she gained more self-confidence and progressed from an emotional downward spiral to an upward spiral. Her personality blossomed. She began dating, and within two years had remarried. Through Christmas cards I'm annually reminded that love, for this woman, is better the second time around.

In the book *The Case Against Divorce*, Dr. Diane Medved also details some additional extremes or exceptional situations when you could justify divorce. A person seriously considering divorce would be well advised to read her book.[13]

However even though there may be one of these circumstances in your marriage, divorce is not inevitable. You might be wise to get out of such a marriage, but don't act too fast.

If your marriage has had quality or still has potential for happiness, give your marriage partner a chance to make a comeback. How much time should we give a floundering loved one? At least months, and sometimes years. But each of us must have the courage to protect our own health and happiness at a crucial point in time. You can save your marriage in most cases if you take the right kind of action to correct the problem.

How to Seek Professional Help
for Your Marriage

In the early stage of trouble, the two of you might remedy harmful behavior by reading about marriage adjustment and by taking classes on mental health and marital health. But if behavior has deteriorated considerably, counseling should be sought.

How do a husband and wife find competent professional help for their marriage? If there are addictions, a drug rehabilitation center is a vital source of help. If one is mentally ill or seriously disturbed emotionally, a psychiatrist, clinical psychologist, or some other reputed psychotherapist should be consulted. When there are marriage problems, it is important that you consult with a counselor who specializes in marriage and family therapy. Most marriage counselors are capable of helping with emotional adjustment problems as well. Although many psychiatrists and psychologists are highly skilled in doing individual counseling, few have had training in marriage and family therapy.

If you and your partner have decided that you need professional help for your marriage, look for a couple therapist who is a Clinical Member of the American Association for Marriage and Family Therapy (AAMFT). This organization is most concerned with the education, training, and licensing of marriage counselors. You should shop much more carefully for a capable marriage counselor and family therapist than you would for expensive clothes and a car.

Counselors vary in their ability to help people. Therefore, you would be wise to inquire beyond the yellow pages. You could ask your physician, clergyman, professor, and even friends for their recommendations.

After you begin counseling, if you are uncomfortable with the counselor, or if he or she does not seem to be helping you, do not hesitate to try someone else. If your marriage counselor is capable, you will begin to learn what to do immediately from this counselor to protect and to improve your marriage. A good counselor is a good teacher and a good coach. A lack of information is one of the cardinal reasons why people become entangled in problems. For health and happiness, a couple needs to be informed pertaining to matters such as nutrition, aerobics, mental health, contraception, sexual response, and conflict resolution.

Beware of a counselor who wants to take a lot of your time and money for delving into the psychodynamics of your childhood. Uncovering factors that might have contributed to a current problem does not remove it. After we have figured out exactly what caused a tire on our car to go flat, the tire is still flat.

One can be a doctor of psychiatry, which requires a medical degree; a psychologist with a PhD; or a social worker with either a masters degree or a doctoral degree. One can become a licensed professional counselor without having been required to take even one class on marriage and family therapy, and yet 80 percent of these professionals say they do marriage therapy according to a major study.

It is essential for you to interview on the telephone or in person any one you are considering hiring to help you and your partner reconcile and magnify your happiness together.

Even if a counselor has been a student in marriage and family classes and is licensed as a marriage and family therapist, there is no guarantee that this person is pro-marriage.

Choose a licensed marriage counselor (a marriage therapist), who has the following qualities:

- One who is pro-marriage and who is in favor of helping most couples reconcile and remain together and create a happier marriage especially when they have young children.
- A marriage professional who has taken university classes on the art of marriage and family therapy.
- One who has had tutoring and training in the art of successful marriage counseling—marriage therapy.

Read the talk given by Dr. William J. Doherty at the Smart Marriages Conference July 3, 1999, *How Therapy Can Be Hazardous to Your Marital Health.* (He teaches and trains doctoral students to become competent marriage therapists.)

There are important questions for you to ask a professional counselor who refers to himself or herself as a marriage counselor or as a marriage and family therapist. When deciding whether to choose this counseling professional to help you and your partner, the first question should be, are you married and do you enjoy being married? How long have you been married to the same man or woman? Do you believe that marriage can be and ideally should be forever? Have you ever been divorced?

What is your college or university background in regard to classes on marriage and the family?

What seminar training have you had and do you plan to continue having to help prepare you to be a proficient, capable marriage counselor or marriage therapist?

Are you licensed as a marriage and family therapist or counselor?

Have you written any books or magazine articles on love and marriage that have been published?

Do you prefer to do marriage counseling by meeting with the husband and wife together? Or would you rather counsel with them separately?

If your professional marriage helper occasionally requests to meet with you separately, this is acceptable and will probably be beneficial for the growth and development of your marriage.

Any professional who says that he or she would prefer to meet with a husband and wife separately for *all* of the counseling should be ruled out. The most effective therapy is accomplished by meeting with the husband and wife together in "the therapeutic triangle."

Judges and lawyers in most divorce proceedings declare in essence that this divorce is necessary because the husband and wife have "irreconcilable differences."

My wife, Eleanor, and I recently celebrated our golden wedding anniversary. I will facetiously explain several ways in which Eleanor and I could be described as having irreconcilable differences.

1. First, our life tempos are exceedingly different. For example, Eleanor is relaxed, kind, and easygoing. In contrast, I am often energetic, impatient, and proactively assertive in my lifestyle and relationships.
2. Eleanor takes naps. She endeavors to persuade me to also take a nap.

3. Eleanor is very conscientious about following the rules; I abide by the rules enough to stay out of jail and am much less concerned about what people might think of me when my behavior could be interpreted as eccentric.

4. My wife thinks the day is over at midnight. I usually remain up past midnight not wanting to miss out on anything interesting.

5. Eleanor seems to think that it is important not to eat before going to bed; I always have a "midnight snack" because I would not want to get hungry while I'm asleep.

6. We have lived in our present house for over ten years. Just after we moved in, I endeavored to persuade Eleanor that we should move the clothes washer and dryer from the kitchen to upstairs near the bedrooms. She prefers that the clothes washer and dryer remain in the kitchen, and so that is where it will be forever.

I hope that these examples might motivate some couples to optimistically look for what is right with their marriages and what is good about their love life together. And realize the importance of their togetherness for the happiness and development of their children and thereby avoid unnecessary divorce.

Remember, couples who play together are more likely to stay together. And church leaders teach that couples who pray together are more likely to stay together. "Together forever, for better or for worse, for richer or for poorer, in sickness and in health."

NOTES

1. Michele Weiner-Davis, *Divorce Busting* (New York: Summit Book, 1992).
2. E. Mavis Hetherington, Martha Cox, and Roger Cox, "The Aftermath of Divorce," in J.H. Stevens Jr. and Marilyn Matthews, eds., *Mother-Child, Father-Child Relations* (Washington: National Association for the Education of Young Children, 1978).
3. Diane Medved, PhD, *The Case Against Divorce* (Ballantine Books 1989).
4. Weiner-Davis, *Divorce Busting*. Michele Weiner-Davis is the founder of DivorceBusting.com.
5. Hetherington, Cox, and Cox. "The Aftermath of Divorce," in *Mother-Child, Father-Child Relations*.

6. Judith S. Wallerstein and Sandra Blakeslee, *Second Chances: Men Women and Children a Decade After Divorce* (New York: Ticknor & Fields, 1990), 225.

7. Judith S. Wallerstein, Julia M. Lewis, and Sandra Blakeslee, *The Unexpected Legacy of Divorce*. (New York: Hyperion, 2000), 138.

8. Robert Rector, "Married Fathers: America's Greatest Weapon Against Child Poverty," June 16, 2010. Web Memo #2934 Institute for American Values, The Heritage Foundation.

9. Maggie Gallagher, "The Stakes Why We Need Marriage," National Review Online, July 14, 2003, http://article.nationalreview.com/269352/the-stakes/maggie-gallagher.

10. Used with permission. CMFCE@smartmarriages.com.

11. L J Waite et al., 2002, Institute for American Values ©

12. Scott Stanley in monograph L J Waite et al 2002, Institute for American Values ©

13. Medved, *The Case Against Divorce*.

22

Answers to Questions People Ask

Can a husband and wife with a wide age disparity have a happy marriage?

Yes, they can. An example is a distinguished former Prime Minister of Great Britain named Benjamin Disraeli. He married a woman named Marry Ann who was fifteen years older than he. Marry Ann knew virtually nothing about history, government, and politics. Nevertheless, they were very happily married for thirty years and remained together until death.

In our marriage, my husband and I want to have a lot freedom as individuals, and yet we want to have a close marriage. Can we have both?

Yes, you can have both, provided the two of you are careful to follow certain guidelines.

I would counsel you as individuals to be honest with yourself; to continue to pursue your own interests within limits, whether these be recreational, social, educational, or career activities; develop your talents; and do not ignore your personal needs.

However, if you want to have a stable, happy marriage, you both must forego some personal desires from time to time. For example, a husband or wife must be willing to readily forego a hunting or skiing trip because of being needed at home. Cooperative assistance in homemaking, child care, university studies, and employment matters all deserve higher priority than personal recreation and entertainment.

One needs to decide at the beginning of marriage to be true to the partner. Socialize in ways that will help you be loyal to each other. Be protective of your relationship but not possessive.

This means it is best to participate in most social activities as a couple, instead of as individuals. Even though you intend to be true to one another, you make it easier for yourselves to be untrue if you habitually socialize with others when your marriage partner is unable to accompany you. Even though you intend to be faithful, it's possible for you to create distrust.

One might be sexually faithful and yet relate to members of the other sex in ways that constitute disloyalty. Partners in love are more likely to be true when each has an expectation of loyalty and makes this clear to the marriage partner. You are both justified and wise to draw a line somewhere to communicate your disapproval of certain social behavior on the part of your husband or wife that you believe might jeopardize the happiness and permanence of your marriage

Is it best to always be totally honest in a marriage? And should you have to confess to each other anything that is on your conscience?

Honesty is the best policy. If you want your partner to trust you, you cannot be honest just half of the time, or most of the time. You must be honest all of the time. None of us would fully trust someone if we knew that person was dishonest some of the time, even though we knew he was honest most of the time.

When one starts lying, his or her honesty deteriorates rapidly. Soon a second lie is needed to cover the first, and a third lie to cover the second one, until the pattern of one's words looks like a roof-top of shingles. Regarding confessions in marriage, a considerable number of married persons seem to be unable to resolve their guilt after committing adultery until a confession is made to the marriage partner. As a marriage counselor, I give my acceptance and emotional support to a client who has decided he needs to make a confession to his mate in order to overcome guilty feelings. However, I do not recommend confession to a spouse as an absolute necessity. In fact, I caution clients against confessing to a marriage partner if it is quite obvious that the mate would respond to the bad news with depression, hate, and retaliation.

If one can reconcile his or her conscience by confession in prayer, or in conference with a church leader or professional counselor, it might be best in some marriages not to inform the marriage partner of a transgression. Being honest does not require that a person must indiscriminately tell everybody everything. Withholding certain information can protect a loved one's feelings and prevent distrust from developing.

What is the easiest way to make a marriage partner change?

You cannot make anyone change, but you can motivate them to want to change.

A circular reactive pattern develops in marriage when one partner's motivates the mate to respond with some other kind of undesirable behavior, and in turn this increases the negative behavior of the first spouse. This kind of circle in the dynamics of a relationship can be symbolically portrayed as the circular pattern of A behavior equals more of B behavior equals more of A behavior.

No husband or wife has an easy way, as with a magic wand, to "make" the loved one change. In his book *Couples*, Dr. Carlfred Broderick gives fascinating examples of deteriorating marriages because of circular reactive behavior. For example, the more time a husband spends away from home, the more his wife nags him about this, and the more she nags him, the more he stays away.

However, these circles are not always characterized by "more equals more equals more," but instead sometimes by "less equals less equals less."

In a joint counseling session, after the wife had complained about her husband's lack of yard work, he issued a counter complaint. *Husband:* "There is something that you're leaving out of this altogether from my point of view." *C.S.:* "Yes, let's hear it." *Husband:* "All right, all the time that she's talking about, 'I won't help her, I won't help her,' she's saying it like I'm just doing it out of orneriness. And basically that's exactly right." *C.S.:* "What do you mean by that?" *Husband:* "All right, the night before I asked her to make love. She said 'no!' That is not going to help my anger a bit. OK, let me ask you something, Doc. If you're gone from your wife for five days and you come home on the sixth day, you'd expect your wife to be just a little happy to see you, wouldn't you?" *C.S.:* "I sure would." *Husband:* "You'd expect your wife to be just a little affectionate? You'd expect that, wouldn't you?" *C.S.:* "Yes, I would. You're telling your wife that you will not help much with the yard work because you are mad at her for repeatedly turning you down?" *Husband:* "No, it wasn't a matter of being mad." *C. S.:* "You're hurt and disappointed?" *Husband:* "That's exactly right. Why should I do anything for her when she won't take time for me?" *C. S.:* "I can understand your feelings." *Wife:* "Usually when he got home it was 10, 11, 12, or 1 o'clock at night. I was dead tired from cleaning the house all day so it would be clean when he came home. And putting up with the kids all week—by Friday night I was tired." *C.S.:* "Most husbands would prefer that a wife would clean the house less vigorously and rest up for lovemaking. If we are going to have an enjoyable marriage, we must take time to rest so we have some energy for love; we must plan and prepare for it. If we only went to work when we are exhausted, we would not like our work. Also, if a husband and wife get together in bed only when they are tired, how much are they going to enjoy each other?"

The action that will break this vigorous circle is for at least one, and preferably both love partners, to yield to the wishes of the other. It's as if each is saying to the other, "I'll improve myself if you'll first improve yourself." Remember, the easiest way to get your partner to change is for you to change first. Once you have taken the initiative in self-improvement, you have gained bargaining power leverage for convincing your partner to also make certain changes.

My fiancé and I are of different religions. Because we are each devout in our own faith, we intend to maintain our present church affiliations. If you believe our marriage can be a success, how can we make the best adjustment in spite of our religious differences?

It might be encouraging to you to know that more interfaith marriages succeed than fail. There are certain realities, however, that you both need to be aware of.

Intense romantic feelings for one another cause certain couples to err in thinking that their religious differences have an insignificant impact on their marriage. Religious differences are insignificant between lovers who do not take religion seriously. But if you are both devout about your different faiths, understanding certain realities about religion can be of help to you.

If you and your fiancé are conscientious about religion and what your churches teach, then the following facts are pertinent to your situation and can help the two of you adjust well to this challenge in your lives.

First, you are what you are to a great extent because of your religion, not in spite of it.

Second, religion is not just something that you do one day a week. It is, instead, an attitude and a way of living your life seven days a week.

Third, an interfaith marriage necessitates more tolerance and adaptability than a marriage of the same religion.

In beginning your marriage with religious differences, keep in mind that you have four adjustment alternatives.

First: conversion. Each of you will do well to carefully consider joining each other's church because religious agreement helps unify a marriage and strengthens a family. This way of adapting is the best provided the conversion is genuine. But if you impulsively change to your mate's church without learning, understanding, and truly believing, your conversion will lack authenticity and you are likely to drift back to your former religion.

You must be honest with yourself and mentally weigh the value that conversion can be to your own life as well as the benefits it can bring to others who are dear to you.

Second: you can each choose to keep your own separate religious affiliations, but the divorce rate is higher among couples who do this compared to marriages in which one converts to the faith of the other. You can do certain things to strengthen your marriage, even though you have a religious difference. Although you do not fully agree on religious doctrines and scriptural interpretations, you can at least socialize together at one another's church. You can participate together in such church events as dinners, dances, receptions, farewells, Boy Scout activities, and holiday parties.

Third: if you have children, one of the most difficult challenges that will confront you will be the decision of which church your children should attend. You must make a choice while your children are very young. Some engaged persons have said their intention is to impart neither the religion of the mother nor the father to the children, but allow them to choose after they reach adulthood. But this is very unrealistic. Children in such families will probably choose the religion they have been taught, namely none.

One could reach a compromise by raising their sons in the church of the father and their daughter in the mother's faith. This arrangement is as fair as possible as far as the children's religion goes; nevertheless, this couple might have disappointments and disagreements in their marriage because of their religious differences.

Regular church attendance and religious teachings contribute to children's moral development and keenness conscience. Therefore, if one spouse is devout and the other is not, it will be best for parents to bring their children up in the faith of the most religious parent.

Some couples will be able to resolve their religious differences by joining a new church together. Doing this will be easiest when neither of them have strong loyalty to their present church and when their theological perspectives are primarily the same. A man and woman, who are members of the Methodist and Congregational Churches, might agree to join the Presbyterian Church. This example is given because there are more similarities among these three churches than differences. When there are no monumental differences between the churches of fiancés, they will find it easier to compromise and unitedly join a new church.

The fourth adjustment alternative in a religiously mixed marriage is for the husband and wife to drop religion entirely. Many couples do this for the purpose of avoiding conflict. But the choice to abandon religion will leave a void in the lives of those who have found it to be meaningful. If you've found religion to be valuable in your life, you are cautioned against this option. One of the other three alternatives is recommended to you instead, especially conversion.

My church teaches against masturbation, but various physicians write that it is physically harmless and some psychologists even recommend it as a means of relieving tension. How should my wife and I teach our children about this?

If you and your family members take your religion seriously, it is important for a clear conscience that each of you endeavor to abide by your church's teachings. As parents you need to think clearly about this and communicate your conclusion to your children.

One of the easiest and most effective ways for you to communicate your values to your children on sexual matters is through books. You will need to peruse books on sex carefully as a means of deciding which ones to purchase or to check out of a library for your children to read. This is necessary because there is a wide variation of values presented in sex information literature.

Although you might be very much opposed to self-pleasuring or autoeroticism, you need to be cautious not to overstate your case or overreact when talking with your teenage sons and daughters, because overreacting when talking with your older sons and daughters about this can induce harmful feelings of guilt. I don't know of any scripture that teaches that masturbation is an extremely serious sin. However, quality sex and happiness in marriage requires a high degree of other centeredness instead of self-centeredness. Autoeroticism is a self-centered practice. If it becomes a strong habit, an individual may find it difficult to discontinue after his or her wedding.

I do not believe that parents or clergymen should be so intrusive as to bluntly ask an adolescent or anyone, "Do you masturbate?" Adults in positions of authority can tactfully impart their values and can give admonitions without personally interrogating. Talk on this topic needs to be depersonalized. For example, a parent or clergyman could communicate to a young adult somewhat as follows: "You probably know that the practice of caressing one's self sexually is called masturbation. Although many individuals do this, I'd like you to understand that our church is opposed to it. We advise against it because it is a self-centered practice and it can become a habit that might detract from the quality of one's future marriage." This manner of communication protects one's privacy and helps maintain rapport in the relationship.

Self-pleasuring paired with pornography can accelerate into obsessive compulsive behavior.

If one is emotionally upset because of an inability to control autoeroticism, this person might find professional counseling with someone who is religiously oriented and also kind and courteous to be helpful.

A twenty-nine-year-old wife in her second marriage asked me, "Why do some husbands masturbate? And what is your opinion of this?"

Many husbands, and a considerable number of wives, do occasionally engage in what I would call autoeroticism, or self-pleasuring. Some do so regularly and others occasionally.

This often takes place with couples who have chronic conflict in their relationship. Another reason is self-centeredness, characterized among certain individuals by a lack of effort to communicate with the partner. Sex is the most intimate kind of communication. Autoeroticism has the potential of becoming habituated and intensified when one is engaging in this practice while viewing or hearing pornographic messages or cybersex (mutual pleasuring email). There are mental health professionals who specialize in treating this kind of behavior.

Although I do not know of any religious teachings that say that autoeroticism is a serious sin, some churches do teach against it especially because of the reasons mentioned. When it is engaged in as a habit, it can weaken a marriage because one's libido—one's sexual desire and energy—is limited. It is very important to share with each other this libidinal energy and pleasure. As previously explained in the chapter on sexual love in your marriage, that sharing creates profound feelings of love and affection between a husband and wife.

Another reason for a spouse to engage in masturbation is that a physical disability may preclude the possibility of sexual intercourse.

In many of these marriages, however, it is still possible for a husband and wife to experience shared orgasm. Along with being an expression of love, sex is also a sharing of intense pleasure. These are two reasons why sex can strengthen a marriage.

Even though a disabled spouse might not be able to engage in sexual intercourse, a couple in such a marriage would do well to make love as often as both find it enjoyable. Their lovemaking can include mutual caressing, which in most cases can bring both husband and wife to sexual climax.

After a couple is married, is it still all right for the husband to have a night out with "the boys" on a regular basis?

Most marriages will be weakened and escalate toward divorce if either the husband or wife repeatedly spends nights out "with the boys" and "with the girls." One who has a strong desire to do this is not yet ready for marriage. This style of socializing can create distrust, and it is fraught with opportunities to be unfaithful. Nevertheless, it is safe enough for a husband and wife to participate as individuals in some recreational activities, but most of their socializing should be together.

How does a wife increase her self-esteem and learn to read signs of approval, love, and admiration from a husband who has difficulty expressing himself?

Whatever we esteem, we value. For happiness we must have self-esteem, which for adults comes mainly from living a good life. The crux of self-respect is within one's self, just as the "city of happiness" is within one's state of mind.

You can encourage your husband to be more expressive by asking his opinion on what you are wearing, or a meal you've prepared, or a paper you've written for a class.

If you often express approval, love, and admiration to him, he will be more apt to respond in like manner. Make it clear to him that you would like to hear more affirmative words, but don't nag him about this communication shortcoming. If he wants to improve by becoming more expressive, he will. He's free to decide. Each morning remind yourself to accept him exactly the way he is. You will accept him more fully if you will decide *now* to have the kind of attitude toward him that is expressed in the song "He's Just My Bill."

How can I reconcile the idea that "for happiness one must find oneself" with the New Testament teaching that "one must lose oneself"?

These two ideas do not really conflict. They both convey a salient message for mental health.

The advice from the ranks of psychology to find oneself is another way of saying, know thyself. After discovering your true characteristics, if you are to be happy, you must accept them wholeheartedly.

The New Testament admonition to lose ourselves is really a caution against selfishness, or at least against too much self-centeredness. Selfishness is a major cause of personal misery as well as marital failure. One who's all wrapped up in himself or herself makes a small package. If one is truly maturing, he steadily reduces the number of his psychological mirrors and converts them into windows; that is, he becomes less self-centered and more "other-centered."

If one is to be happy after finding and accepting oneself, he must learn to love himself properly. Keeping oneself physically strong, mentally alert, and morally straight is loving oneself properly. Drug abuse, nutrition neglect, ugly language, books and movies that pollute one's mind, and deviating from one's code of morality by certain behaviors are all violations of what psychology and religion teach about mental health.

How much influence should parents expect to have on a child who is grown and married? And how much influence should the adult child permit the parent or parent-in-law to have on the marriage?

If married partners have a good relationship with their parents, then they are fortunate if they live near their parents, because family members can be of great help to each other. When families of loved ones live close, there can be an ongoing interchange of assistance and companionship. Care of houses, yards, and children can be cooperatively accomplished. Grandparents can read to children, tutor them, and impart their philosophies of life to them. One's judgment in many cases is deepened and tempered with the passing of years.

What about older parents and grandparents who live a considerable distance away? Their contribution to the lives of their adult children can be maintained by letters, recordings, telephone calls, and emails. Older parents need to be invited and encouraged to "come visit often." They might be reluctant to visit because of not knowing that they are welcome, or because of thinking they might be a bother or that they are too old to travel. Because of not being in school or employed, grandparents generally can leave their homes to visit for an extended length of time with fewer complications than can younger families. It is reasonable for relatives of younger and older families to relate to each other as closely and as often as they find to be mutually beneficial and enjoyable

If you begin to think that certain relatives are intruding too much into your life, then have the courage to communicate your thoughts and feelings honestly to these individuals. Each of us needs a degree of privacy and time free from others. We all need to remember that family members can become tired of our company, even though they love us very much.

Can television and other media threaten the happiness of a marriage and family?

Television and other electronic media can bring more good than bad into a home if family members are willing to compromise and exercise self-discipline in limiting their time watching TV, texting, accessing the Internet, social networking, watching movies, and listening to music. Cyber affairs are an extreme threat to the health and happiness of a marriage.

Adults can be a good example by watching and using media for education and by using entertainment media in moderation. Screening, limiting time, and supervising are essential for managing quality use of electronic media.

Death, divorce, crime, bullying, and sex are examples of topics that can be brought up and discussed with teenagers when they have seen this on television. Questions can be answered, and thoughts and feelings shared, on topics such as these during commercials. Television can facilitate personal development and can strengthen family relationships if it is managed wisely.

If a husband is out of work and decides now is the time to go back to college, should a wife go to work to help him obtain his goal, particularly when children under the age of five years will be involved?

It is important for your husband to get the education he needs to get the type of employment he will enjoy and that will provide a good living for your family. There are certain things that you can do to facilitate your children's optimum development while you are employed and your husband is in school.

If you have relatives nearby who are willing and able to be daytime parent substitutes, consider requesting their assistance. Offer to pay your family members just as you would anyone else performing child-care services for you. If no relatives live close, inquire of certain friends concerning their interest in assisting with the care of your children. Your kids will adjust more quickly if they are cared for by someone whom they already know. If no friends or relatives are available, be careful to interview a considerable number of applicants and get references before finalizing your choice to employ someone to care for your children.

You need someone who will do more than just care for your children.

You must find someone who will also help your children

develop their minds and personalities. This requires someone who enjoys talking and reading to children.

If you are renting, consider moving into college housing or very near the campus where your husband will be attending school. This will make it possible for him to help care for the children when he has time between classes. Knowing that their father is attending school nearby can give a feeling of security to your children.

If you are considering a day-care center or pre-school program, it's very important that you investigate carefully. You have the right to visit a center or school several times and request letters of recommendation as a means of helping you and your husband make a wise decision.

My husband leaves the care and development of our children mainly up to me. What can I do to get him more involved in their lives?

Buy your husband a book on how to be a good dad. *Father Power*, by Henry Biller and Dennis Meredith, is an excellent book, and *The Father's Almanac* is well recommended. Reading books like these can help a man understand the vital role that fathers play in the development of daughters as well as sons.

If you are expecting, invite and encourage your husband to attend classes on prenatal care with you. If you live in or near an urban center, there are probably evening classes on parenthood in which you can both enroll. After an inquiry, if you learn there are no such classes in your vicinity, talk with your husband about the possibility of forming a parenthood discussion group. Meeting in such a group only once a month could ignite your husband's interest and help both of you improve your parenting skills. As a group you could select a certain book to read and discuss, such as *Surviving With Kids* by Wayne Bartz and Richard Rasor.

You can help your husband become more active as a father by often handing him the baby to hold or to feed, frequently asking him to bathe the baby or young children, and having him read the children a bedtime story. Be fair enough to trade chores with him when he's caring for the children. Remember to express appreciation when he participates in the care and development of your children.

Can the name which parents select for their child affect his or her development?

For good mental health, it's important that a child not have a name that makes him self-conscious. There is evidence that a person's success and happiness can be influenced by how that individual feels about his or her name. Names evoke certain stereotypes, some ego building, and some demoralizing, according to S. Gray Garwood, a developmental psychologist. One of his studies shows that students with widely accepted names were more popular with teachers and tended to do better in school. If a child senses that others, especially teachers, respond negatively to him, it hurts his feelings and weakens his self-confidence.

Research conducted by Dr. Herbert Harari, a psychologist at San Diego State University, has led him to conclude that children with particularly unusual names are often taunted by classmates and are less likely to be popular.[1] Another research project showed a comparatively higher percent of persons with unusual names being arrested or receiving psychiatric treatment.[2]

Dr. Robert C. Nicolay and Dr. Arthur A. Hartman, Chicago psychologists, compared unusual names from court psychiatric clinic files with an equal number of more conventional names such as James, Elizabeth, David, John, Joseph, and Mary. They found more than four times as many psychotic individuals in the group with very unusual names. "Those with peculiar names admitted readily that their names had been a source of constant embarrassment," says Dr. Nicolay. "After all, a child's future personality must grow within the shadow of his name, and most children tend to identify with the strength or weakness in their names."[3]

Dr. Nicolay also notes that "If a child is to be satisfied with his or her name it should be easy to pronounce and spell, must not summon undesirable nicknames, and should not be so different as to evoke constant comment."[4]

What is most important is for you to avoid choosing a name that will make your child feel self-conscious either because of its connotation, or because it's a nuisance to pronounce or spell. However, feel free to select names that are unusual if you prefer, but be careful to avoid those which are peculiar or extremely different. Two unusual women's names that I like are Janel and Amber.

Consider carefully how well a given name goes with the family surname.

Eric is a very popular name nowadays but it does not go well with a family name such as Herrick. I know a family whose last name is Baum. If they were to name a son Adam, he might not like this combination, even though Bible names are now quite popular.

In too many cases, parents gratify their own ego instead of thinking about what their child would probably prefer. I'm referring to parents who tack their own first name in front of the name that they call their child. For example, a father named Paul Jones names his son Paul Michael Jones. He and his wife call their son Mike. Michael will probably find a letter "P" in front of the name he goes by to be a nuisance, and it can be inconvenient for others who are trying to look up his telephone number or identify him for some reason.

In addition, parents impose an unnecessary inconvenience on a child when they decide to spell the name slightly different than the usual spelling, such as Tresa instead of Teresa or Lezlee rather than Leslie. This will require a child to have to spell his name and explain it to others a million times.

I think there is some advantage for an individual when the name indicates clearly that this person is either male or female. This can help a child achieve sex identity—that is, identify with members of his or her own sex, and could elicit a more positive response from one's peers, particularly during childhood. Examples of names that parents tend to give to both sons and daughters are Marion, Francis, and Sydney.

If a child is self-conscious about his name, or if he finds it to be a nuisance, his parents should consider allowing him to use a nickname or even to select a new name. Books and articles have been written to give parents guidance on this subject.

As a newlywed couple who plans to have children, what can we do to help our children be happy and successful?

Newborn babies are able to sense their parents' feelings and usually develop the same kinds of feelings. If you want your child to be happy and enjoy life, *you first* must be happy and know how to enjoy life. Decide now that you are going to enjoy your baby and each of your children. One of the most important things that you'll ever do for them is to enjoy them.

It has been said that one of the best things a man can do for his children is to love their mother. If this is true, it follows that one of the best things a woman can do for her children is to love their father. Every family has a certain "emotional tone." In each home the predominate mood of the family may be described with such terms as hostile, oppressive, anxious, indifferent, sad, supportive, optimistic, cheerful, and loving. Think about how the emotional tone in your family is affecting the happiness at your children.

To esteem means to value. We value and have high regard for that which we esteem. It is essential that a child or any human being have self esteem. This will be initiated by how you, as parents, relate to him or her. We want children to value themselves and to value virtually all people. We as parents do not want our children to be arrogant, egotistical, and inappropriately proud. The Old Testament cautions against self-destructive pride, and the New Testament advises us not to think more highly of ourselves than is appropriate.

Giving frequent doses of *focused* attention to your baby and children is a way of saying, "I like you and you're important to me." When we give focused attention to someone, we communicate face to face and listen attentively. Even while feeding, bathing, and dressing a baby, parents can give focused attention by looking at and talking to him or her. This is far more likely to give a child a feeling of being loved than merely hearing glib statements of love that are tossed out without feeling. In her book *Your Child's Self-Esteem,* Dorothy Briggs explains how focused attention from parent to child builds self-esteem and heightens rapport.

A child is more likely to esteem himself, that is value himself, if we, the parents, help him develop his potential. Beginning soon after birth, parents can do much to help a child's mind and personality develop. The more often parents take time to read to and talk with their children, beginning even in babyhood, the more likely these children will become bright and charming. *A Parent's Guide to the First Three Years* by Professor Burton White explains how important this talking and reading is for the development of a child's intellect and personality.

Enrolling your child in a good nursery school or preschool for four to ten hours a week, starting at about age three, can be extremely valuable in strengthening his or her mental and social abilities. Be careful to compare a number of preschools before you select one for your child. Visit various schools and talk with some of the parents who've already enrolled their children in these schools before you make your choice. The teacher of the school is the most important factor. Be certain she has the academic background to conduct a nursery school and be reasonably sure that she has the kind of personality that will enrich your child's personality.

Because of the importance of the early years, the amount of money that you spend for preschool could take your children much further in their development than the same amount of money that might be later spent for their college education. Having been a university professor, I'm certainly in favor of a college education, and I want to emphasize how crucial the early years are in a child's development. However, neither nursery school nor college is absolutely necessary for your child's happiness and success. For happiness, our children must learn to love as well as be loved, and they must learn to live their lives productively.

Courtesy, kindness, and respect from parents to children will strengthen their self-esteem and contribute to their happiness. A habit of making put-downs or of looking at a child condescendingly is not only discourteous, but also damaging to his feelings of self-worth. In all our human relations, we need to learn to do more purring and less snarling.

A child is sensitive to what his peers think of him or her. Therefore, it's especially important that we are kind to him when he is in the company of his friends. Have the courtesy to introduce your children whenever you meet a friend or an acquaintance that they do not know. Since children learn by example, they are more likely to respect their parents if their parents first respect them, and courtesy is an important ingredient of respect.

A child is more likely to have self-esteem and be happy:

1. If he knows he is loved.
2. If we avoid ridiculing him for his fears and mistakes.
3. If we forgive him for his mistakes and help him learn to forgive himself.
4. If we provide for him a wide range of experiences and help him acquire knowledge and skills.
5. If we help him become his best but teach him to avoid thinking he must be "the best" in all aspects of life.
6. If we help him see himself and accept himself as he really is, yet motivate him to make improvements.

Let's remember that self-esteem is essential for happiness and success and that during your children's early years, you, as parents, mainly determine their self-esteem or lack of it. But the older they become, the more responsible they are for creating their own self-esteem. As one grows beyond early childhood, his feelings about himself are increasingly created by how he lives his life. An adult's lifestyle determines almost fully how he feels about himself. If you clarify this truth to your children as they grow older, you will bolster their ability to live their lives in a manner which will bring well deserved self-esteem and happiness.

NOTES

1. Jean E. Lard, "Why You Shouldn't Name Your Child 'Jughead' (and other poor choices)," *Parade Magazine*, December 21, 1980.
2. "Your Child's Name Could Mark Him for Failure," in *Ladies Home Journal*, June 1970, 137.
3. Ibid.
4. Ibid.

Do's and Don'ts

Do say often to your marriage partner, "I love you."

Don't ever say "I hate you."

Do be slow to anger and avoid expressing strong anger.

Don't remain in the same room if both of you are starting to fall apart at the anger seams.

Do go into another room or go outside and walk briskly with an understanding that you will return home as soon as you calm down.

Don't follow your marriage partner when she or he has expressed a desire to depart temporarily.

Do often express affection by caressing and by complementing.

Don't continue trying to talk with each other when one or both of you are starting to erupt with volcanic anger.

Do take time be romantic—to often reromanticize your marriage.

Don't ever think that you don't have time to be romantic or that you are too old for that.

Do make love often with your marriage partner, so you both can experience euphoria about being in love with each other.

Do remember good sex is a lubricant for your marriage machinery.

Do often turn toward your marriage partner.

Don't turn away from your partner unless you are doing it strategically for anger control.

Do be pro-marriage by planning to be together forever.

Do reminisce often about highlights in your courtship and marriage.

Do write love letters to each other often.

Don't use the D-word—divorce—when you and your partner are having a tiff.

Do be of good cheer.

Don't grumble and complain.

Do speak warm words.

Don't speak cold cutting words.

Do compliment often.

Don't criticize with blame.

Do remember to shut up when you realize you have said enough.

Don't think you have to get in the last word even when you know you are right.

Do develop friendships with other happily married couples.

To protect the stability and happiness of your marriage, **don't** affiliate most of the time with couples who are very unhappy in their marriages and with individuals who are divorced.

Do continually read good books on how to have a happy marriage.

Do understand and accept the fact that praying, reading scriptures, and attending church together can protect and strengthen your marriage and family.

Don't naively endeavor to invalidate the truth of the previous statement.

Do remember that sexual love will magnify your marital happiness. One major reason for this is it results in the release of "feel good chemicals."

Don't weaken your marriage by neglecting to regularly reromanticize.

Do forgive your marriage partner for his or her imperfections.

Don't ever withhold affection and sexual love from your marriage partner for the purpose of punishing him or her.

Do remember that couples who play together stay together.

Don't burden your marriage with drudgery by being workaholics.

Do remember that your home is the place where you live and love and laugh.

Do be of good cheer and remember the importance of a sense of humor. Laughter is the shortest distance between two people. When you realize you and your partner are arguing about trivia, ask yourself, is this the hill I want my marriage to die on?

Do appreciate and respect the important differences between men and women—between masculinity and femininity.

Do remember that "Love changes everything, how we live and how we die." —Andrew Lloyd Webber

Affirmations to Magnify the Love and Happiness in Your Marriage

IT IS IMPORTANT that you and your marriage partner often read these statements aloud together.

CHARITY—I am loving my partner with charity, the purest kind of love.

Charity includes qualities such as being courteous, kind, and respectful and being compassionate and sympathetic.

I know that love is an attitude and a set of actions.

It is how I think about someone and how I treat that person.

I can love anyone I decide to love.

Every day I will renew my decision to love my marriage partner.

COMMITMENT—I will be true to my partner and will cooperate in creating and re-creating happiness together.

COMPANIONSHIP—We work and play together and share most of our experiences.

COMMUNICATION—We reveal most of our thoughts, feelings, hopes, and plans to each other; also our needs, wishes, and desires.

We take time to listen and to reflect back what was said. We build up one another

We speak more positives than negatives; more compliments than criticism; more affirmations than negations and put-downs.

In our relationship we give more warm fuzzies than cold pricklies. We do more purring than snarling.

AFFECTION—We are affectionate in our marriage. We express our affection by gentle touching and by speaking words of endearment.

ANGER—We protect our relationship by controlling anger and letting go of it.

We know how to resolve disagreements and conflicts.

REPENTANCE AND FORGIVENESS—In our relationship we have "Bounce Back Ability" because we often repent and forgive.

We know that to repent means to change and to improve.

ROMANCE AND COURTSHIP—We creatively enhance the romance in our marriage.

We often cooperate to reromanticize our relationship.

EROTICTONICS—We frequently revitalize our relationship with sexual love.

ENJOYMENT, FUN, AND LAUGHTER—Are an important part of our marriage.

ECONOMIC STRENGTH—We are becoming stronger financially because we buy carefully and we make wise business decisions. We are informed, trained, and skilled for occupational success.

Recommended Books

Couples: How To Confront Problems and Maintain Loving Relationships, Dr. Carlfred Broderick

Couple Skills, Matthew McKay, et al.

Fighting for Your Marriage, Howard Markman, Scott Stanley, et al.

Light His Fire, Ellen Kreidman

The Ten Second Kiss, Ellen Kreidman

Take Back Your Marriage: Sticking Together In a World That Pulls Us Apart, William J. Doherty, Ph.D.

The Sex-Starved Marriage—Boosting Your Marriage Libido: A Couple's Guide, Michele Weiner-Davis

The Proper Care & Feeding of Marriage, Dr. Laura Schlessinger

The Seven Principles for Making Marriage Work, John M. Gottman, PhD, and Nan Silver

Between Husband and Wife, Stephen Lamb and Douglas Brinley.

About the Author

D<small>R. C</small>LARK S<small>WAIN</small> is a marriage and family counselor and a psychotherapist in Boise, Idaho, with over thirty years of teaching and counseling experience. He is a clinical member of the American Association for Marriage and Family Therapy and is a licensed marriage and family therapist and a licensed clinical professional counselor.

Clark Swain graduated with honors with a degree in marriage, family, and human development and earned his PhD degree in marriage and family counseling from Florida State University.

Dr. Swain is the author of the bestselling book *Enriching Your Marriage*. He has also written many articles on love and marriage that have been published in the *Ensign* and *New Era* magazines.

He was a distinguished Professor of the Year Award nominee and was a professor of marriage and family life at Montana State University and at Boise State University. He has also been a guest professor at nine universities.

Dr. Swain calls his counseling service in Boise, Idaho, the Marriage Enrichment Center. He specializes in marriage counseling, sex therapy, and divorce busting.

He and his wife, Eleanor, have been married for over fifty years, are the parents of five children, and have seventeen grandchildren.

Visit his website at www.marriageboise.com.